Beyond the Framework
of Modern Thought

by Seymour Lessans

Beyond the Framework of Modern Thought

Seymour Lessans

Published by Safeworld Publishing Company, 2021.

Table of Contents

Philosophy – Free will and determinism. 2. Good and Evil

3. Peace–Psychological aspects. 4. Interpersonal relations.

5. Psychology — Popular works. 6. Lessans, Seymour — Philosophy.

ISBN: 978-1-954284-91-3 (Epub)

ISBN: 978-1-954284-00-5 (Paperback)

ISBN: 978-1-954284-02-9 (Adobe PDF)

There is an audio that goes along with this book. You can listen to a sample as the author reads and elaborates on Chapter One. Just copy the link below and scroll down.

www.declineandfallofallevil.com/ebook[1]

Safeworld Publishing Company

TO ALL MANKIND

This is the most fantastic non-fiction book ever written because it will verify the prediction made in the introduction by producing unbelievable changes in human relations. By discovering the invariable laws of the <u>solar system,</u> we were able to predict an eclipse and land men on the moon. By discovering the invariable laws that inhere in the <u>mankind system,</u> we are able, for the very first time, to predict and accomplish what was never before possible—our deliverance from evil.

Please note that when the 20th century is mentioned, it refers to the time this finding was first uncovered. The prediction that in 25 years man would be delivered from all evil was based on the conviction that a thorough investigation would already have taken place. Although it has been more than 60 years, there has been no such investigation, and until today, this discovery remains in obscurity. Although some of the author's references are dated, the knowledge itself couldn't be timelier.

INTRODUCTION

WHO... IN HIS RIGHT mind or with a knowledge of history, would believe it possible that the 20th century will be the time when all war, crime, and every form of evil or hurt in human relations must come to a permanent end? When first hearing of this prophecy, shortly after Hitler had slaughtered 6 million Jews, I laughed with contempt because nothing appeared more ridiculous than such a statement. But after 15 years (8 hours a day) of extensive reading and thinking, my dissatisfaction with a certain theory that had gotten a dogmatic hold on the mind compelled me to spend nine strenuous months in the deepest analysis, and I made a finding that was so difficult to believe, it took me several years to thoroughly understand its full significance for all mankind.

I tried to get several professors to let me explain what I had discovered, but such a world was so far removed from their own knowledge and capabilities that they looked at me as if I was a crackpot. But I couldn't be angry because I was the same way before I made my discovery. And the theologians I contacted, though they admitted they pray to God for deliverance from evil, also believe it is impossible for man to accomplish this apparent miracle. Humorously enough they are right in a way because the law that was discovered is equivalent to the law that inheres in the solar system, over which we have no control. This natural law, which reveals a fantastic mankind system, is the long-awaited Messiah. It was hidden so successfully behind a camouflage of ostensible truths, that no wonder it wasn't found until now. But by demonstrating the power of this law, a catalyst, so to speak, is introduced which compels this fantastic change in the direction our nature has been traveling, performing what will be called miracles, though they do not transcend the laws of nature.

Laugh if you will, because your skepticism is normal, but your smile of incredulity will be wiped from your face once you begin to read the text, chapter by chapter, of which the first two are most fundamental. Just bear in mind how many times in the course of history has the impossible (that which appeared to be) been made possible by scientific discoveries, which should make you desire to contain your skepticism enough to investigate what this is all about. It was Nageli, the leading authority of his time, whose pride refused to let him investigate the claims of Gregor Mendel whom he judged a semi-amateur because he regarded as impossible the very core of Mendel's discovery. But he was wrong as history recorded, and though Mendel was compelled to receive posthumous recognition for the law he discovered, he is now considered the father of modern genetics. So don't be too hasty to use your knowledge and intellectual capacity as a standard to judge what hasn't even been revealed to you yet. But when it is, should you decide to give me the benefit of the doubt, deny it and two other discoveries to be revealed, if you can.

BEYOND THE FRAMEWORK OF MODERN THOUGHT

SEYMOUR LESSANS

CHAPTER ONE
THE HIDING PLACE

MANY YEARS AGO, MAN formed a theory that this earth was flat because he could not conceive of it floating in space. It became a dogma, such a fixed idea that when the first astronomer wished to explain the reason why a darkness came over the sun in the middle of the day, he was denied an opportunity to present his findings because the hiding place of his discovery called into question this sacred belief. How dare anyone say the earth is round!

You may look back and smile at the unconscious ignorance of our ancestors, but pay close attention to what happened to me as I draw up a perfect comparison with which you can identify.

Because I had considered my discovery completely scientific, my attention was drawn to an article by Eric Johnston, who is now deceased but was then, among other things, the President of the Motion Pictures Association. It appeared in the November 6, 1960, issue of This Week Magazine of The Baltimore Sun.

"If there is one word which characterizes our world in this exciting last half of the twentieth century, the word is change.

"Change in political life... change in economic life... change in social life... change in personal life... change in the hallmark of our times. It's not gradual, comfortable change. It is sudden, rapid, often violent. It touches and often disrupts whole cultures and hundreds of millions of people.

"Behind it all lies an explosive growth in scientific knowledge and accomplishment. Some 90 percent of all the scientists who ever lived are living today, and the total accumulation of scientific knowledge is doubling every ten years.

But this is reality. If we remember that, then we will never flinch at change. We will adjust to it, welcome it, meet it as a friend, and know it is God's will."

Since my discovery would bring about the greatest change in all of history, it appeared that this man would be willing to let me explain my findings. By convincing him on the phone that it was now possible to put a permanent end to all war as a result of my discovery, he agreed to meet me on a Sunday afternoon in Washington, D.C. Our conversation went as follows:

"I'm really not a scientist, Mr. Lessans, and in all probability, you should be talking to someone else. Besides, after you hung up, I became more skeptical of claims such as yours because they not only sound impossible but somewhat ridiculous in view of man's nature. I don't mind listening if it won't take too long. I do have another engagement, but I can devote at least one hour."

"I will be as brief as possible, but in order for me to reveal my discovery, it is absolutely necessary that I first show you its hiding place because they are related to each other. You see, Mr.

Johnston, most people believe, consciously or unconsciously, that man's will is free . . ."

"What's that! Did I hear you correctly? Are you trying to tell me that man's will is not free?"

"That is absolutely true, Mr. Johnston, and my discovery lies locked behind the door marked Man's Will is Not Free, just like the invariable laws of the solar system were concealed behind the door marked The Earth is Round — until some upstart scientist opened it for a thorough investigation."

"Your door was opened many times through the years, Mr. Lessans, by some of the most profound thinkers, and never did they come up with any discoveries to change the world."

"It is true that determinism was investigated by people who were presumed profound thinkers, but in spite of their profoundness, none of them had the capacity to perceive the law that was hidden there."

"I don't know what it is you think you have discovered, but whatever it is, as far as I personally am concerned, it cannot be valid because I am convinced that man's will is free. Thank you very much for coming out, but I'm not interested in discussing this matter further."

Now stop to think about this for one moment. A discovery has been made that will go down in history as that which will change the entire world of human relations for the better, yet because it lies hidden behind a theory that 98% of mankind are compelled to believe true, there is a hostile reaction when it is questioned. Where is there one iota of difference between this attitude and that of our ancestors regarding the shape of the earth? One person actually said to me, "What difference does it really make what I think about free will and determinism?

My opinion can never change what our will really is." This is true enough, but if the will of man is definitely not free, isn't it obvious that just as long as we think otherwise, we are prevented from discovering those things that depend on this knowledge for their discovery; consequently, it does make a difference. The opinion of our ancestors that the earth was flat could never change its actual shape, but just as long as the door marked The Earth Is Round was never opened thoroughly for an investigation by scientists capable of perceiving the undeniable but involved relations hidden there, how were we ever to discover the laws that allow us now to land men on the moon? Therefore, it is necessary to point out that I am not going to reveal a theory or an opinion about how this new world will come into existence but will give a scientific demonstration, and your awareness of this will preclude the possibility of someone adducing the rank of his title or the long tenure of an accepted belief as a standard from which he thinks he qualifies to disagree with anything that contains within itself undeniable proof of its veracity. In other words, your background, the color of your skin, your religion, the number of years you went to school, no matter how many titles you hold, your I.Q., your country, what you do for a living, your being some kind of expert like Nageli (or anything else you care to throw in) has no relation whatsoever to the undeniable knowledge that 3 is to 6 what 4 is to 8.

Will Durant opened the door to the vestibule of determinism and then, after looking around, wrote: "Let the determinist honestly envisage the implications of his philosophy," which indicates that all his reasoning in favor of free will was the result of inferences derived from the inability of logic to accept the implications. What are these implications that made him also write: "If there is an almost eternal recurrence of philosophies of free will, it is because direct perception can never be beaten down with formulas, or sensation with reasoning." What made it so obvious to him that man's will is free, and why do theologians treat this as if it is an undeniable reality?

The belief in free will came into existence out of absolute necessity, not only so theology could relieve God of all responsibility for evil since he was considered good, but primarily because it was impossible for man to solve his problems without blame and punishment, which required the justification of this belief in order to absolve his conscience. In other words, if you were called upon to pass judgment on someone by sentencing him to death, could you do it if you know his will is not free? To punish him in any way, you would have to believe that he was free to choose another alternative than the one for which he was being judged; that he was not compelled by laws over which he had no control. Man was given no choice but to think this way, and that is why our civilization developed the principle of an "eye for an eye and a tooth for a tooth," and why my discovery was never found. No one could ever get beyond this point, because if man's will is not free, it becomes absolutely impossible to hold him responsible for anything he does. Well, is it any wonder the solution was never found if it lies beyond this point? How is it possible not to blame people for committing murder, rape, for stealing, and the wholesale slaughter of millions? Does this mean that we are supposed to condone these evils; and wouldn't man become even less responsible if there were no laws of punishment to control his nature? Doesn't our history show that if something is desired badly enough, he will go to any lengths to satisfy himself, even pounce down on other nations with talons and tons of steel? What is it that prevents the poor from walking into stores and taking what they need, if not the fear of punishment? The belief that will is not free strikes at the very heart of our present civilization. Is it any wonder that Johnston did not desire to go into this matter further? Right at this point lies the crux of a problem so difficult of solution that it has kept free will in power since time immemorial. However, before I demonstrate how it is possible to resolve the implications, it is necessary to know that I will proceed in a step-by-step manner that brooks no opposition. Therefore, the first step is to prove undeniably that whatever your reasons for believing free will true cannot be accurate because it is impossible to prove this theory since proof requires turning back the clock, so to speak, and demonstrating that man could have chosen otherwise. Since there is no way we can reverse the order of time, the most we can do is assume that he didn't have to do what he did. We justify our assumption by saying – "He didn't have to do it if he didn't want to," which is one hundred percent true, but there is no way we can prove that his desire could have been otherwise at that moment of time. This means (now pay close attention to this simple equation) that if it is impossible to prove free will true, it is also impossible to prove determinism (as the opposite of free will) false, because if determinism was proven false, this would prove free will true, and we just demonstrated that this is impossible unless we can turn back the clock. But this doesn't stop a person from saying, "I believe. It is my opinion.

I was taught that man's will is free," but it would certainly stop him from trying to defend his position with an argument. However, once it is proven conclusively that will is not free (which takes into consideration the implications), there can be no more opinions or theories expressed on the subject, just as our ancestors stopped saying, "I believe the earth is flat," once they knew for a fact it was round.

There is a great deal of humor here because the philosophers who did not know it was impossible to prove freedom of the will, believed in this theory because they were under the impression their reasoning had demonstrated the falseness of determinism, which was just shown cannot be done. Yet Will Durant, not perceiving this relation, wrote: "For even while we talked determinism, we knew it was false." This is why it is necessary to proceed in an undeniable, not logical manner; otherwise, someone will quote Durant, a priest, professor, lawyer, judge, or politician, as an authority for believing in freedom of the will. Remember, we are not interested in opinions and theories regardless of where they originate, just in the truth, so let's proceed to the next step and prove conclusively, beyond a shadow of doubt, that what we do of our own free will, of our own desire because we want to, is done absolutely and positively not of our own free will.

In reality, we are carried along on the wings of time or life during every moment of our existence and have no say in this matter whatsoever. We cannot stop ourselves from being born and are compelled to either live out our lives the best we can or commit suicide. Is it possible to disagree with this? But since it is absolutely impossible to be both dead and alive at the same time, and since it is absolutely impossible to desire suicide unless dissatisfied with life (regardless of the reason), we are given the ability to demonstrate a revealing and undeniable relation.

Every motion, from the beating heart to the slightest reflex action, from all inner to outer movements of the body, indicates that life is never satisfied to remain in one position for always like an inanimate object, which position shall be termed death. I shall now call the present moment of time or life – here, for the purpose of clarification, and the next moment coming up – there. You are now standing on this present moment of time and space called here and are given two alternatives: either live or kill yourself; either move to the next spot called there or remain where you are without moving a hair's breadth by committing suicide. If you are still reading, then it is obvious that you are not satisfied to stay in one position, which is death or here, and prefer moving off that spot to there, which motion is life. Consequently, the motion of life, which is any motion from here to there, is a movement away from that which dissatisfies; otherwise, had you been satisfied to remain here or where you are, you would never have moved to there. Since the motion of life constantly moves away from here to there, which is an expression of dissatisfaction with the present position, it must obviously move constantly in the direction of greater satisfaction. But let me elaborate on this.

Supposing you were taken prisoner in wartime for espionage and condemned to death, but mercifully given a choice between two exists: A is the painless hemlock of Socrates, while B is death by having your head held under water. Is it humanly possible, providing no other conditions are introduced to affect your decision, to prefer exit B if A is offered as an alternative? But if your will is free, you should be able to choose B just as well as A. The reason you are confused is because the word choice is very misleading, for it assumes that man has two or more possibilities, but in reality this is a delusion because the direction of life, always moving towards greater satisfaction, compels him to prefer of differences what he considers better for himself, and when two or more alternatives are presented, he is compelled, by his very nature, to prefer not that one which he considers worse, but what gives every indication of being better for the particular set of circumstances involved. The purpose of choosing is to compare meaningful differences to decide which alternative is preferable. A and B, representing small or large differences, are compared. The comparison is absolutely necessary to know which is preferable. The difference considered favorable, regardless of the reason, is the compulsion of greater satisfaction desire is forced to take, which makes one of them an impossible choice in this comparison simply because it gives less satisfaction under the circumstances. Consequently, since B is an impossible choice, man is not free to choose A.

Just because some differences are so obviously superior in value where you are concerned that no hesitation is required to decide which is preferable, while other differences need a more careful consideration, doesn't change the direction of life, which moves always towards greater satisfaction. The truth of the matter is that all through life, man is under a compulsion to choose what he considers good for himself, but what one person judges good or bad for himself doesn't make it so for others, especially when it is remembered that a juxtaposition of differences in each case present alternatives that affect choice. Now just take careful note of this simple reasoning that proves conclusively in another way, except for the implications already referred to, that will is not free.

Man either doesn't have a choice because none is involved, as when something happens to him; or he has a choice and then is given two or more alternatives, of which he is compelled, by his nature, to prefer the one that appears to offer the greatest satisfaction, whether it is the lesser of two evils (both considered bad for himself), the greater of two goods, or a good over an evil. Therefore, it is absolutely impossible for the will to be free because man never has a free choice. However, it is important to understand that the words good and evil, in this context, have reference only to what is a benefit or a hurt to himself. Killing someone may be good in comparison to the evil of having that person kill him. The reason someone commits suicide is not because he is compelled to do this against his will, but only because the alternative of continuing to live under certain conditions is considered worse. He was not happy to take his own life, but under the conditions he was compelled to prefer, by his very nature, the lesser of two evils which gave him greater satisfaction. Consequently, when he does not desire to take his own life because he considers this the worse alternative as a solution to his problems, he is still faced with making a decision, whatever it is, which means that he is compelled to choose an alternative that is more satisfying. For example, when the alarm clock goes off, he has three possibilities: commit suicide so he never has to get up, go back to sleep, or get up and face the day. Since suicide is out of the question under these conditions, he is left with two alternatives; but even though he doesn't like his job and hates the thought of going to work, he needs money, and since he can't stand having creditors on his back or being threatened with lawsuits, the lesser of two evils is to get up and go to work. He is not happy or satisfied to do this when he doesn't like his job, but he finds greater satisfaction doing one thing than another. Dog food is good to a starving man when the other alternatives are horse manure or death, just as the prices on a menu may cause him to prefer eating something he likes less, even though he has the money, because the other alternative of paying too high a price for what he likes more is still considered worse under his particular circumstances. The law of self-preservation demands that he do what he believes will help him stay alive and make his life easier, and he is willing to cheat, steal, kill, and do any number of things which he considers good for himself in comparison to the evil of finding himself worse off if he doesn't do these things.

Great confusion arises when man uses the words, "I did it of my own free will," for although it is impossible to do anything of one's own free will, he does everything because he wants to since absolutely nothing can make him do what he doesn't want to. Was it humanly possible to make Gandhi and his followers do what they did not want to do when unafraid of death, which was judged, according to their circumstances, the lesser of two evils? Consequently, when any person says he was compelled to do what he did against his will, that he really didn't want to but had to because he was being tortured, he is obviously confused and unconsciously dishonest with himself and others because he could die before being forced to do something against his will. What he actually means is that he didn't like being tortured because the pain was unbearable, so rather than continue suffering this way, he preferred, as the lesser of two evils, to tell his captors what they wanted to know, but he did this because he wanted to, not because some external force made him do this against his will. If, by talking, he would know that someone he loved would be instantly killed, pain and death might have been judged the lesser of two evils. This is an extremely crucial point because, though will is not free, absolutely nothing on this earth can make man do anything against his will. To repeat, he might not like what he did, but he wanted to do it because the alternative gave him no free or better choice.

And now I shall demonstrate how these two undeniable laws or principles – that nothing can compel man to do anything against his will because, over this, his nature allows absolute control; and that his will is not free because his nature also compels him to prefer of available alternatives the one that offers greater satisfaction – will reveal a third invariable law – the discovery to which reference has been made.

CHAPTER TWO
THE TWO-SIDED EQUATION

NOW ONCE IT IS ESTABLISHED as an undeniable law that man's will is not free, as was just demonstrated, we cannot assume that it is free because philosophers like Durant cannot get by the implications. Therefore, we must begin our reasoning where he left off, which means that we are going to accept the corollary – THOU SHALL NOT BLAME – even though it presents what appears to be an insurmountable problem, for how is it possible not to blame people who hurt us when we know they didn't have to do this if they didn't want to? Because Spinoza didn't understand the full significance of this enigmatic corollary, though he accepted it by rejecting the opposite principle of an eye for an eye, he refused to defend himself against his sister or blame her for cheating him out of his inheritance. Neither had a free choice because the one was willing to cheat to get what she wanted, while he was willing to be cheated rather than hold her responsible. But the time has arrived to clear up all the confusion and reconcile these two opposite principles, which only requires that we keep an open mind and proceed with the investigation. However, let me show you how this apparent impasse can be rephrased in terms of possibility.

If someone is not being hurt in any way, is it possible for him to retaliate or turn the other cheek? Isn't it obvious that in order to do either, he must first be hurt? But if he is already being hurt and, by turning the other cheek, makes matters worse for himself, then he is given no choice but to retaliate because this is demanded by the laws of his nature. Here is the source of the confusion. In other words, our basic principle or corollary, Thou Shall Not Blame (call it what you will), is not going to accomplish the impossible. It is not going to prevent man from desiring to hurt others when not to makes matters worse for himself, but will prevent the desire to strike the very first blow. Spinoza made matters worse for himself financially, but at that moment of time he had no free choice because it gave him greater satisfaction to let her cheat him out of what he was entitled to by law. Christ also received incursions of thought from this same principle, which compelled him to turn the other cheek and remark as he was being nailed to the cross: "They know not what they do," forgiving his enemies even in the moment of death. But they knew what they were doing, and he could not stop them even by turning the other cheek. In all these years, no one has ever known what it means that man's will is not free, but you will be shown the answer very shortly. In reality, everybody is and has been obeying God's will – Spinoza, his sister, Nageli, Durant, Mendel, Christ, and even those who nailed him to the cross, but God has a secret plan that is going to shock all mankind. This new world is coming into existence not because of my will, not because I made a discovery (sooner or later it had to be found because the knowledge of what it means that man's will is not free is a definite part of reality), but only because we are compelled to obey the laws of our nature.

Do you really think it was an accident the solar system came into existence; an accident that the sun is just the proper distance from the earth so we don't roast or freeze; an accident that the earth revolves just at the right speed to fulfill many exacting functions; an accident that our bodies and brains developed just that way; an accident that I made my discovery exactly when I did? To show you how fantastic is the infinite wisdom that controls every aspect of this universe through invariable laws that we are at last getting to understand, which includes the mankind as well as the solar system, just follow this: Here is versatile man – writer, composer, artist, inventor, scientist, philosopher, theologian, architect, mathematician, chess player, prostitute, murderer, thief, etc. – whose will is absolutely and positively not free despite all the learned opinions to the contrary, yet compelled by his very nature and lack of development to believe that it is since it was impossible not to blame and punish the terrible evils that came into existence out of necessity; and then permitted to perceive the necessary relations as to why will is not free and what this means for the entire world, which perception was utterly impossible without the development, and absolutely necessary for the inception of our Golden Age. In all history, have you ever been confronted with anything more incredible?

We have been growing and developing just like a child from infancy. There is no way a baby can go from birth to old age without passing through the necessary steps, and no way man could have reached this tremendous turning point in his life without also going through the necessary stages of evil. But be this as it may, the confusion of words and the inability to perceive certain type relations has compelled many people to believe that if man knows his will is not free, it would give him a perfect opportunity to take advantage of this knowledge and shift his responsibility. He could just say, "I couldn't help myself because my will is not free." But let us observe what the perception of undeniable relations tells us.

If you know, as a matter of positive knowledge, that we are not going to blame you or question your conduct, is it possible for you to blame us, to extenuate the circumstances, to lie, or try to shift your responsibility in any way? Isn't it obvious that the answer must be "no, it is not possible," just as the same answer must apply to the question, is it possible to make two plus two equal five?

This proves conclusively that the only time you can say, "I couldn't help myself because my will is not free," or offer any kind of excuse, is when you know you are being blamed, for this allows you to make the effort to shift your responsibility. This means that only in a world where you are judged, where it is believed your will is free, can you use an excuse to justify what you do. It also means that you must assume complete responsibility for everything you do since you cannot shift it away from yourself under the changed conditions. Did you ever see anything more ironically humorous? The only time you can use the excuse that your will is not free is when we believe it is free, but when you know that we will never blame or judge you in any way, you cannot use that or any other excuse to shift your responsibility. We have been so confused by words in logical relation that while we preach this freedom of the will, we say, in the same breath, that we couldn't help ourselves, and demonstrate our confusion still more by believing that the corollary would lessen, when instead it increases our responsibility.

"But," this same confusion may inquire, "why can't man just satisfy his desires to his heart's content when he knows there will be no consequences or explanations necessary?"

Has it been forgotten already that we are compelled, by our nature, to choose the alternative that gives us greater satisfaction, which is the reason our will is not free? Consequently, to solve this problem, it is only necessary to demonstrate that when all blame and punishment are removed from the environment, and when the conditions are also removed that make it necessary for us to hurt others as the lesser of two evils, the desire to hurt them will be the worst possible choice. In other words, the knowledge that there will be no consequences presents consequences that are still worse, making it impossible to consider this hurt as a preferable alternative. If will was free, we could not accomplish this simply because we would be able to choose what is worse for ourselves when something better is available, but this new law of our nature, soon to be revealed, will give us no alternative when we are forced to obey it in order to derive greater satisfaction. Let me show you what I mean.

At this moment of time in our present world of free will, you are trying to decide whether to hurt us in some way, but you have had everything removed that could be used to justify this act. You simply see an opportunity to gain at our expense, but should you decide against it, you will not be a loser. In other words, you are considering the first blow, which simply means that you are planning to do something to us that we don't want done to ourselves.

You realize there is a certain risk involved, if caught, because you must face the consequences. But if the crime, misdemeanor, or offense is not that serious, although you know you will be questioned and blamed, you may be able to get away with it by offering all kinds of reasonable excuses as to why you had no choice. But if there is no way any excuse is acceptable as in a court of law after you have been found guilty, or when your parents, boss, or any others know that you are obviously at fault, you could be sent to prison, electrocuted, hanged, gassed, spanked, severely punished in some other way, scolded, reprimanded, ostracized, criticized, discharged, beat up, or any number of things. You don't want this to happen if it can be avoided, but if you can't satisfy your desire unless the risk is taken, you are prepared to pay a price for the crime of hurting others with a first blow.

Under these conditions, it is impossible for your conscience to exercise any control over your desires, simply because you can't feel any guilt just as long as you are prepared to suffer the consequences. But observe what miracle happens when the two laws mentioned in the last paragraph of the first chapter are brought together to reveal a third law.

As before, you are trying to decide whether to hurt us in some way, but you have had everything removed from which you might have been able to justify your act. You simply see an opportunity to gain at our expense, but you will not be a loser if you decide against it. You are contemplating the first blow under changed conditions.

BEYOND THE FRAMEWORK OF MODERN THOUGHT

You know, as a matter of undeniable knowledge, that nothing in this world has the power, that no one can compel you to do anything against your will, for over this you know you have absolute control (you can lead a horse to water, but you can't make him drink). This means that you are completely responsible for your actions, even though, due to circumstances, you may prefer hurting us. But to make absolutely certain that you know this is an undeniable law, try to shift your responsibility to us or some extraneous factor when you know that no one in the world will ever hold you responsible. It cannot be done, which was already proven. This does not mean that other people are not often responsible for the hurt we do as part of a chain reaction, as when an employer is forced to lay off his employees because the money to pay them has stopped coming in to him, but no one is blaming him for what is obviously not his responsibility, and therefore it isn't necessary for him to offer excuses.

Now here you are contemplating this hurt to us in some way, while we know, as a matter of positive knowledge, that you cannot be blamed anymore because it is an undeniable law that man's will is not free. This is a very unique two-sided equation, for it reveals that while you know you are completely responsible for everything you do to hurt us, we know you are not responsible. For the very first time, you fully realize that we must excuse you because it is now known that man must always select of available alternatives the one that offers greater satisfaction, and who are we to know what gives you greater satisfaction? This prevents you from thinking excuses in advance because you know you are already excused. You can't say, "I couldn't help myself because my will is not free," because you know we already know this. You can't apologize or ask forgiveness because you are already forgiven, and no one is blaming you. This means that should you decide to hurt us with this first blow or be careless and take the risks that lead to a first blow, and we would have to choose between retaliating or turning the other cheek, you would know that we would be compelled by our nature to find greater satisfaction in turning the other cheek because of the undeniable fact that we would know you had no choice since your will is not free. But remember, you haven't hurt us yet because this is still under consideration, and when it fully dawns on you that this hurt to us will not be blamed, judged, or questioned in any way because we don't want to hurt you in return for doing what must now be considered a compulsion beyond your control — although you know it is not beyond your control at this point since nothing can force you to hurt us unless you want to — you are compelled, completely of your own free will (to be humorous), to relinquish this desire to hurt us with a first blow because it can never give you greater satisfaction under the changed conditions. In other words, it becomes the worst possible alternative to take advantage of not being blamed for a first blow because there is no advantage in hurting those whom you know must turn the other cheek for their satisfaction. Conscience, your guilty feeling over such an act, will not permit it simply because you will get less satisfaction, not more. Now let me review this.

In order to hurt another, man must be able to derive greater, not less satisfaction, which means that self-preservation demands and justifies this, that he was previously hurt in some way and finds it preferable to strike back an "eye for an eye," which he can justify also, or else he knows, absolutely and positively, that he would be blamed by the person he hurt and others if they knew. Retaliation is a natural reaction of a free will environment that permits the consideration of striking the first blow because it is the price man is willing to risk or pay for the satisfaction of certain desires. But when it is removed so the knowledge that it no longer exists becomes a new condition of the environment, then the price he must consider to strike the first blow is completely out of his reach because, to do so, he must choose an alternative that is less satisfying, which is impossible to do when an alternative offering greater satisfaction is available. The answer to this impasse, which removes the implications, is now very obvious because the advance knowledge that man will not be blamed for the first blow since his will is not free (when he knows that nobody, absolutely nothing, can compel him to do this unless he wants to, for over this he knows he has absolute control), enters a condition or catalyst never before a permanent factor in human relations, as this prevents those very acts of hurt for which blame was previously necessary as a normal reaction in the direction of greater satisfaction. However, to fully understand the fact that conscience (our feeling of guilt) was never allowed to reach the enormous temperature necessary to melt our desire to even take the risk of striking a first blow, it is only necessary to observe what must follow when a crucible is constructed wherein this new law can effectively operate.

It should be obvious that just as long as man is able to justify hurting others, he is not striking a first blow. But before I demonstrate how this justification is permanently removed, and to allow you an opportunity to see exactly what happens in a human relation where this is already removed, I shall reveal, in the next chapter, how all automobile accidents must come to a permanent end.

CHAPTER THREE
AUTOMOBILE ACCIDENTS

TO UNDERSTAND WHY ALL automobile accidents must come to an end out of absolute necessity, I shall show you exactly what takes place in our present environment before and after a collision, and then let you see the same accident under changed conditions.

Actually, the only reason we are willing to drive carelessly and take risks is simply because when we do have an accident, which means that when we have made a careless mistake resulting in a hurt to others, it is possible to gain satisfaction by paying the price or shifting our responsibility. When it becomes impossible to do either, we must do everything in our power to prevent the accident as that alternative which is better for ourselves.

NOT LONG AGO, A TRUCK was heading west inside the city limits doing 50 miles an hour in a 35-mile zone. It was past midnight, and very few cars were on the street. The driver was anxious to get home because he hadn't seen his family for a week. He had driven this same route many times and knew it was safe to go this speed at that time of the morning. His only concern was to keep an eye out for a patrol car so he wouldn't get a ticket. Up ahead, four blocks away, he saw that a traffic signal was green. When about one-half block away, he knew that it would soon be joined with the yellow light and followed, in a few seconds, by the red, indicating that he would have to stop. But since this was a nuisance, since the amber light had not yet gone on, and since the darkness enabled him to see that no headlights were coming from other directions, he felt safe to increase his speed to 65 miles an hour.

But heading north was a car carrying five people. A father, mother, and their three children. They had just attended a wedding and were on their way home. The father had been drinking rather heavily and completely forgot to put on his headlights. He was also traveling along at 50 miles an hour when he slowed down to 35 so he wouldn't have to stop for the red light up ahead, but when he saw the yellow light go on for the other direction, and knowing that the light would be green before he entered the intersection even if he resumed his 50 miles an hour, he didn't hesitate to do just that. Now just before the truck got to the crossing, the light changed, which meant that the driver would have to go through on the red, and at that very moment he saw the car without any headlights on enter the intersection a fraction of a second ahead of him, but it was too late to avoid the collision. The father saw the truck at that instant, too. They both jammed on their brakes and turned their wheels instinctively, but the truck ploughed head-on, at a slight angle, into the rear right side of the car. The parents were somehow only injured slightly, the truck driver was not hurt at all, but the three children were killed instantly. Standing on the corner was someone who noticed that the car's lights were not on. Now, let us analyze this.

If the truck driver had any inkling that such an accident would have resulted from his trying to beat the light, he certainly would never have considered it, but he chose to do what he did because it gave him greater satisfaction at that moment. However, we are not concerned now with what he should or shouldn't have done, but with what he must do for greater satisfaction following this accident. It is obvious that he feels absolutely horrible over what he knows was his fault, yet he doesn't want to be blamed for the death of these children. There is certainly no satisfaction in feeling the weight of this responsibility; consequently, he is going to do everything in his power to shift it away from himself.

The police arrive and learn that the father was driving without headlights on and that he was highly intoxicated. The truck driver kept saying over and over again – "It was not my fault. That man went right through the red light and didn't even have his lights on. The death of those children is terrible, but it was not my fault." Before long, he was absolutely convinced that the accident would never have occurred had the headlights been on, and he was right because what made him speed up to beat the yellow light was his certainty that no car was coming. However, he could not tell the police the truth because the right-of-way still belonged to the father, even though intoxicated and without lights, but it made him feel so much better.

In court, the father was found guilty of manslaughter even though innocent, which infuriated him, but because the death of his children was considered punishment enough, his sentence was suspended, and he was placed on probation. His wife, however, was not satisfied with the decision since she believed him guilty of killing their children (she had warned him time and again about his drinking at parties) and got a divorce. The truck driver was awarded quite a bit of money in damages because he discovered that he was not physically the same after such a traumatic experience. If he felt the least bit guilty over causing the death of these children, he could always confess this sin to his priest or psychiatrist or atone for it in various ways.

Had the conditions been slightly different, making it impossible for the truck driver to shift his responsibility, the only avenue open for greater satisfaction would have been for him to pay a price for what he did. His insurance would have compensated the parents to a degree for their tragic loss, and they would have been satisfied to know that he was sent to prison. When released, he would feel that he paid a price for what he did. The father, on the other hand, who was found guilty when completely innocent, builds up tremendous hate for the whole system of justice and may desire to kill the truck driver in retaliation if he thinks he can get away with it. His life was ruined, and he wants to hurt somebody in the worst way for what was done to him. Had this accident not taken anyone's life, the driver of the truck might have volunteered that it was his fault so he could compensate this family for their inconvenience and property damage through his insurance company, which allows him to pay this kind of price for hurting others. Now pay close attention to the same accident under changed conditions, so you can see why the truck driver, when faced with the choice of speeding up or slowing down, is compelled to prefer the latter, which prevents the accident.

The truck driver feels absolutely horrible over what he knows was his responsibility, but he also knows that no one in the entire world will ever blame him. The police will not come by in an effort to determine who was responsible. There is no more liability insurance to help pay a price for hurting others. The father is not going to attack the truck driver or say to him, "Look at what you did to my children," even though he and his wife are crying bitterly. But let us take a long look at the truck driver to see how he is making out.

He knows, beyond a shadow of doubt, that the accident was his responsibility because the father entered the intersection on the green light. He can't say to the police or the parents that it was not his fault, because they are not going to blame him in any way. He knows that nothing in this world has the power to make him do anything he doesn't want to do, because over this he has absolute control, and when it fully dawns on him that the parents must excuse what he cannot justify because he knows he was to blame (the two-sided equation), when he fully realizes that he cannot shift his responsibility in any direction whatsoever because nobody is holding him responsible, and that he cannot pay a price for the same reason, he finds himself in a situation from which it is impossible to derive any satisfaction whatsoever. This means that he is compelled to go through life with the death of these children, the sorrow of the parents, and the destruction of their property on his conscience. How do you think he feels? Wouldn't it be wonderful for him if he was punished or could pay a price? But let's examine this from another point of view.

Supposing the father didn't see the truck at all and wasn't certain of what happened. He might actually believe that his drinking was responsible, that maybe it was the fact that he didn't put on his lights or that he did go through the red light, and how do you think he feels knowing that his carelessness might have caused the death of his own children? How will he ever know that he is not responsible unless he is fully aware at all times of what he's doing? This means that the thought of hurting others is so terrifying when there will be no blame, punishment, or price to be paid for what we know is, or might have been, our responsibility, that when we are confronted with a similar situation as the truck driver, we could never find greater satisfaction in speeding up, while the father, knowing that drinking might cause him to get in an accident, figures out a way to solve his problem so he can still drink without taking on the responsibility of driving. But if he has no one to drive his car but himself and feels that drinking might cause an accident for which he knows, well in advance, there will be no blame, he cannot afford the risk of placing himself in a position from which his conscience will torture him all through life.

The right-of-way system in the new world becomes a mathematical standard by which each motor vehicle operator is forced to judge only himself when an accident occurs. The truck driver knows he did not have the right-of-way and therefore struck the first blow when the collision took place. But if he had gotten to the red light and no cars were coming, he would be striking no blow had he decided to cross the intersection. By the same reasoning, his speed is controlled not by a patrol car being present or absent but by what he considers safe enough so that he will never have to encroach on another driver's right-of-way. He can't afford to drive with bad tires or brakes because if the one should blow out and the other fail, forcing him to collide with other cars by entering their territory, he will know that he struck the first blow regardless of the reason. If the tires were new but the mechanic failed to tighten the bolts on one wheel which came off, causing the accident, his conscience would be clear since this was something that happened to him. But the changed conditions will force every mechanic to be extremely careful so they are not responsible for accidents.

Before we will desire to drive a car in the new world, we will want to know everything that might make us responsible for hurting people in an accident which will not occur, and for delaying them from getting to their destination. If by not using directional signals when required (which does not include using them when we are alone on the street or in a lane that only goes to the right or left), or by not moving over far enough when making a turn, we see that we are holding up traffic for which we are not being blamed by the blowing of horns, we will soon find greater satisfaction in not doing anything to hold up traffic. As for whether we need permission from the government to drive...

In our present environment, we do, because many of us are irresponsible. But in the new world our responsibility increases to its maximum degree, and we won't be too anxious to sit behind the wheel until we know we can drive without causing accidents or delays. This means that the Department of Motor Vehicles will be displaced because we will never have to prove to anyone but ourselves that we are qualified to drive and our vehicles in good condition. The fact that certain inadequate standards were set up for others to determine our qualifications only allowed many unqualified people to assume they were qualified because they passed the required test. Even driving instructors in school will never tell us when they think we are ready. Why should they assume this responsibility? They will simply teach us all the causes of accidents and delays, show us how to handle a car properly, and then let us decide when we think we're ready to drive without hurting anyone. However, to launch this new world and create the environment necessary to prevent accidents, wars, crimes, and all the other forms of hurt that plague our lives is a separate problem which will be solved in a later chapter.

This belief in free will and the concomitant blame are equivalent to the thrust of a rocket in getting a satellite into space, for without it we could never have reached the outposts of this Golden Age. But just as the astronauts shed their excess baggage when their rocket has expended its energy in reaching orbit, so likewise will we shed this theory and all the blame that helped us reach this tremendous turning point in our lives.

Well, is it any wonder I titled my book as I did when the solution actually lies beyond the framework of modern thought and cannot even be understood in terms of our present knowledge? There are no precedents. If you are a little less skeptical and more willing to continue the investigation, I shall reveal my second discovery which will play a very important role in the new world.

BEYOND THE FRAMEWORK OF MODERN THOUGHT

CHAPTER FOUR
WORDS, NOT REALITY

JUST AS MY FIRST DISCOVERY was not that man's will is not free but the knowledge reveals by opening that door for a thorough investigation, so likewise, my second discovery is not that man does not have five senses but what significant knowledge lies hidden behind that door.

Someone whose interest had never been sufficiently aroused to pursue my discoveries because they sounded ridiculous, was visiting an exposition in Canada where he saw a sign on one pavilion that read – "Come inside and let us prove scientifically that the eyes are not a sense organ." He was absolutely amazed because he knew that was my reason for saying man did not have five senses, and after returning home became very much involved in my work. However, I have my own proof, so let us get on with what is necessary to open our minds to the fresh air of undeniable knowledge.

The word "sense" is defined as "any receptor or group of receptors, specialized to receive and transmit external stimuli as of sight, taste, hearing, etc." But this is a wholly fallacious observation where the eyes are concerned because nothing from the external world impinges on the optic nerve as stimuli do upon the organs of hearing, taste, touch, and smell. It is an undeniable fact that light travels at a high rate of speed, but great confusion arises when this is likened to sound, as you will soon have verified.

Did you ever wonder why the eyes of a newborn baby cannot focus to see what exists around him, although the four senses are in full working order? It is assumed that the muscles of the eyes have not yet developed sufficiently to allow this focusing, but such is not the case. In fact, if an infant, immediately after birth, was placed in a soundproof room with his eyelids removed and kept alive for fifty years on a steady flow of intravenous glucose, if possible, without allowing any stimuli to strike the other 4 organs of sense, this baby, child, young, and middle-aged person would never be able to focus the eyes to see any objects existing in that room, no matter how much light was present or how colorful they might be, because the conditions necessary for sight have been removed and nothing from the external world impinges on the optic nerve to cause it. Light is one of the conditions of sight. We simply need it to see.

This focusing of the eyes takes place for the first time when a sufficient accumulation of sense experience (hearing, taste, touch, and smell – these are doorways in) awakens the brain, which then desires to see the source of the experience by focusing the eyes as binoculars. The eyes are the windows of the brain through which experience is gained not by what comes in, but by what is looked at in relation to the afferent experiences of the senses. What is seen through the eyes is an efferent experience.

Our scientists, becoming enthralled over the discovery that light travels approximately 186,000 miles a second and taking for granted that five senses was equally scientific, made the statement, which still exists in our encyclopedias, that "if we could sit on the star Rigel with a very powerful telescope focused on the earth, we would just be able to see the ships of Columbus reaching America for the very first time." But once again, they confused certain things, and all their reasoning, except for light traveling at a high rate of speed, was completely erroneous. They made the assumption that since the eyes are a sense organ, it is obvious that light must reflect an electric image of everything it touches, which then travels through space and is received by the brain through the eyes. What they are trying to make us believe is that if it takes 8 minutes for the light from the sun to reach us, it would take hundreds of years for the reflection of Columbus to reach Rigel, even with a powerful telescope. But why the telescope? Let me show you how confused this particular group of scientists really are.

They reasoned that since it takes longer for the sound from an airplane to reach us when 15,000 feet away than when 5000, and since it takes longer for light to reach us the farther it is away when starting its journey, light and sound must function alike in other respects, which is false, although it is true that the farther away we are from the source of sound, the fainter it becomes, as light becomes dimmer when its source is farther away. But the sound from a plane, even though we can't see it on a clear day, will tell us it is in the sky. But why can't we see it if an image is being reflected towards the eyes on the waves of light? The answer is very simple. An image is not being reflected. We can't see the plane simply because the distance reduced its size to where it was impossible to see it with the naked eye, but we could see it with a telescope. We can't see bacteria either with the naked eye, but we can through a microscope. The actual reason we are able to see the moon is simply because there is enough light present, and it is large enough to be seen. The reason the sun looks to be the size of the moon, although much larger, is simply because it is much much farther away, which is the reason it would look like a star to someone living on a planet the distance of Rigel. This proves conclusively that the distance between someone looking and the object seen has no relation to time, simply because images are not traveling towards the optic nerve on the waves of light; therefore, it takes no time to see the moon, the sun, and the distant stars. In fact, if someone on Rigel had a telescope powerful enough to see me writing this very moment, he would see me at the exact time that you would, sitting right next to me, which brings us to another very interesting point.

If I couldn't see you standing right next to me because we were living in total darkness since the sun had not yet been turned on, but God was scheduled to flip the switch at 12 noon, we would be able to see the sun instantly, at that very moment, although we would not be able to see each other for 8 minutes afterwards. The sun at 12 noon would look exactly like a large star, the only difference being that in 8 minutes we would have light with which to see each other, but the stars are so far away that their light diminishes before it gets to us. We don't need light around us to see the stars, nor would we need light around us to see the sun turned on at 12 noon. To sum this up – just as we have often observed that a drum corps is marching out of step to the beat when seen from a distance, because the sound reaches our ears after a step has been taken, so likewise, if we could see someone talking on the moon via a telescope and hear his voice on radio, we would see his lips move instantly but not hear the corresponding sound for approximately 3 seconds later, simply because the sound of his voice is traveling 186,000 miles a second, but our gaze is not, nor is an electric image of his lips impinging on our optic nerve after traversing this distance. But let me prove in still another way that the eyes are not a sense organ.

Line up 50 people who will not move, and a dog, from a slight distance away, cannot identify his master. If the eyes were a sense, if an image was traveling on the waves of light and striking the optic nerve, then he would recognize his master instantly, as he can from sound and smell. In fact, if he was vicious and accustomed to attacking any stranger entering the back gate at night, and if his sense of hearing and smell were disconnected, he would have no way of identifying his master's face, even if every feature was lit up like a Christmas tree, and would attack. This is why he cannot recognize his master from a picture or statue, simply because nothing from the external world is striking the optic nerve, but the question arises: why can man accomplish this? The answer will be given shortly.

Now the knowledge reveals thus far, although also hidden behind the door marked, Man Does Not Have Five Senses, is not what I referred to as being of significance. Frankly, it makes no difference to me that the eyes are not a sense organ, that our scientists got confused because of it, and that a dog cannot identify his master from a picture. But what does mean a great deal to me when the purpose of this book is to demonstrate how it is now possible to remove every bit of evil (hurt) from our lives is that one of the greatest forms of injustice still exists because we have never understood our true relation with the external world, which is related to what we think we see with our eyes. What is this injustice? It is to be judged an inferior production of the human race because of physiognomic differences, and this judgment takes place the moment we call one person beautiful and another ugly, handsome and homely, good-looking and bad-looking. What makes someone remark, "It's a darn shame she got killed; she was so pretty," indicating that the tragedy was greater because of this prettiness? What makes parents give their children nose and teeth operations, if not to increase their physiognomic value? What makes someone good-looking, cute, adorable, lovely, gorgeous, beautiful, handsome? Don't we see these differences with our very eyes? "We do," you might reply, "but beauty is in the eyes of the beholder," which reveals our confusion still more, since this expression does not negate the existence of ugliness, just observes a difference of opinion regarding the type of features that constitute what is beautiful and ugly. To prove what I mean, could you possibly call Miss America ugly or the Wicked Witch beautiful? You might disagree with someone as to which girl in a beauty contest should be judged the winner, but none would be considered ugly. To be classified as homely is the greatest injustice, yet every time we use the whole range of words expressing good looks, we do that very thing. In reality, nobody is beautiful or ugly, just different. But let me show you how these words developed and why they must become obsolete. First, however, let us observe how our brain operates.

At a very early age, it not only records sound, taste, touch, and smell, but photographs the objects involved, which develops a negative of the relation, whereas the brain of a dog is incapable of this. When he sees the features of his master without any accompanying sound or smell, he cannot identify because no photograph was taken. But a baby, having already developed negatives of relations that act as a slide in a movie projector, can recognize at a very early age. To understand this better, let us observe my granddaughter learning words.

As her eyes are focused on a dog, I shall repeat the word dog rapidly in her ear. When she turns away, I stop. This will be continued until she looks for him when hearing the word, which indicates that a relation between this particular sound and object has been established and a photograph taken. This is exactly how we learn words, only I am speeding up the process. Before long, she learns cat, horse, car, chair, door, kitchen, television, airplane, moon, stars, nose, teeth, eyes, hair, girl, boy, and so on. She also learns the names of individuals. Mommy, Daddy, Linda, Janis, Marc, Madeline, Seymour, Oscar, Harold, Monroe, Ida, David, etc. Until she learns the word cat, she could very easily point to a dog when hearing that word because a negative of the difference has not yet been developed, just as a fox cannot be differentiated from a dog until a photograph of the difference has been developed. By the same reasoning, the word Chinese develops not only a negative of differences but of similarities; consequently, when someone is not acquainted with the differences that exist among this race, he only sees that they resemble each other. But if he would live among them and separate them by their individual names, he would soon see their differences and not their similarities. Seeing similarities is what takes place when someone does not learn colors properly, and he is called colorblind when in reality, he is word blind. Of course, if he can't see a difference before learning the words, then he is colorblind. But in the majority of cases, colors are learned in a haphazard manner, and if a blue negative was developed when looking at a subtle shade of green, he will see blue, just as you would see something blue through blue glasses, even though the object was green. If you were taught one word "orange," which included within that symbol a grapefruit and tangerine, you would hand me any one of the three if I asked for an orange, but when you learn the other two words which photographs the difference, then you could not hand me a tangerine or grapefruit if I asked for an orange. My granddaughter can identify her mother from hundreds and hundreds of photographs because the difference is a negative that not only reveals who her mother is, but who she is not.

Now, once it is understood as an undeniable law that nothing impinges on the optic nerve, even though the pupils dilate and contract according to the intensity of light, it becomes possible to separate what exists in the external world from that which is only a negative or word in our head. The belief in five senses made it possible to imagine light waves hitting an object and then reflecting an image to the eyes, for this appears logical, but how is it possible for light to reflect a value that doesn't even exist in the external world? Let me show you how this was accomplished.

From the time we were small children, our relations, parents, friends, and acquaintances have expressed their personal likes and dislikes regarding things that definitely exist in the external world. The words beautiful, pretty, cute, adorable, handsome, etc., heard over and over again with an inflection of pleasure as to the way somebody looks, took a picture of the similarities between this type of physiognomy, and developed negatives which also contained the degree of feeling experienced. As time went on, a standard was established which separated good looks from bad looks, and a whole range of words heard over and over again, with an inflection of displeasure as to the way somebody looks, took a picture of the similarities between this type of physiognomy and developed negatives containing the degree of feeling experienced below this line of demarcation. Not knowing what his brain had done, man was convinced that these similarities he saw with his very eyes actually contained a lesser value than the opposite similarities. He didn't know that his brain had reversed the process by which these negatives were developed and then projected onto the screen of undeniable differences a value that existed only in his head. Let me give you an example of this by using a movie projector.

Here is a smooth white wall with nothing on it, in a dark room. I am dropping a negative plate or slide into the projector, flipping the switch, and just take a look; there is a picture of a girl on the wall. But go up and touch her. All you feel is the wall itself because the girl is not there. Now, we have been doing the same thing with our brain regarding values. The differences in substance were not only divided up by the use of words like man, woman, child, etc. but became a screen upon which we were able to project this value. Drop a negative plate or word slide in your brain projector and flip the switch. Well, just take a look, there is now a beautiful girl, a homely man, an ugly duckling! Turn off the switch (remove the negative plate or word slide) and all you see are the differences in substance because the projected values have been removed. Since we were taught that the eyes receive and transmit sense experience on the waves of light, it was impossible to deny that this beautiful girl was a part of the real world, and when we changed the standard hidden in the word, all we did was change the screen. By saying that this person may not be beautiful physically but has a beautiful soul, we were allowed to see ugly souls as if they, too, existed externally. However, when these negatives of external value are removed, this doesn't stop us from seeing differences that appeal to us more, but instead of saying, "She is the most beautiful girl I have ever seen," which places other girls in a stratified layer of lesser value, we are compelled to say, "She appeals to me more than any girl I have ever seen," which makes it obvious that the value we see exists only for us. The first expression requires that ugly girls exist because certain type features are considered superior, while the second expression only observes that other girls appeal to us less, which makes everybody equal in value except to particular individuals. By removing all the synonyms that describe people as good-looking, nobody is hurt, but by removing all the antonyms that have been judging half the human race as bad-looking, this entire group is raised to an absolute level of equality. And are we given a choice when to continue using these words after we have learned the truth only reveals our ignorance, for which we will never be blamed? How is it possible to criticize people for believing the earth is flat, man's will is free, and his eyes a sense organ, when we know for an absolute fact that they have never learned the truth?

It is true, however, that we are so conditioned by these words that even their removal will not make us like someone more who appeals to us less, but when children are brought up without ever hearing these words, there is no telling to whom they might be attracted without being adversely judged. There are many more words that will go by the wayside, but you will learn of these in a later chapter. We have actually been compelled to look at each other through a kaleidoscope of negatives that transformed us realistically into what we were not. Every other word we used stratified external differences and similarities, which could not be denied, into external values that appeared realistic because they were seen with the direct perception of our sense of sight. Let us now see what change must take place as we extend the knowledge of what it means that man's will is not free and his eyes not a sense organ into the problem of the sexes before marriage.

SEYMOUR LESSANS

CHAPTER FIVE
PREMARITAL RELATIONS

THE FIRST BLOW OF THE sexes is struck when a boy and girl are encouraged and then rejected by the person with whom they have fallen in love enough to desire marriage. More people have had their heart broken and cut out with the knife of unrequited love than is imaginable, but I must remind the reader that our basic principle cannot prevent the impossible. It cannot prevent a girl or boy from rejecting the other, no matter how much the other is in love, when not to do this makes matters worse for them, as would be the case if this necessitated that they reject the person with whom they are in love and who loves them, or that they reject the possibility of meeting someone with whom they could fall in love as much as they are now being loved. But it can prevent the desire to take risks that get them into this kind of situation, where it is necessary to reject the person in love, just as it prevents them from desiring to take risks that lead to automobile accidents. To have loved and lost may be better than never to have loved at all, but this is the lesser of two evils and presupposes that there must always be a contest wherein someone loses and gets hurt, which is completely false.

SEYMOUR LESSANS

Now the word love symbolizes a conscious or unconscious desire in varying degrees for a sexual relation of some kind, and this is easily proven by the fact that it is impossible for a boy and girl to be attracted to someone no matter how physically appealing this individual might be considered, if they know in advance that this person was born without sexual organs, which knowledge makes them aware that this anomaly of nature is incapable of giving or receiving sexual satisfaction. This means that before sexual intercourse takes place, the degree with which one could fall in love is determined by the degree with which the desire to possess a particular person in the ultimate act, as in marriage, is encouraged. In other words, unless a possibility exists that a boy and girl could eventually have some kind of sexual relation, they could never fall in love with each other. Could you fall in love with a photograph of a dead girl? If she was alive, and you know that she would never go out with you, she is dead as far as you're concerned, just as a movie actress would be if there was no possibility of your dating her. Likewise, you could never fall in love with a girl if you know she would never let you touch or kiss her in any way, which only verifies the definition. Consequently, the moment a boy and girl hold hands and kiss, they are, to that degree, encouraging each other towards the possibility of something more and more until some kind of sexual relation is reached, towards the possibility of falling more and more in love. But the meaning of love after marriage or sexual intercourse takes place is a horse of another color, for the intensity of this desire to continue possessing the other depends solely on the degree of sexual satisfaction, which proves conclusively that the stronger the passion, the greater will this feeling of love be, and further demonstrates why there is so much adultery. Most couples remain together after physical satisfaction has sunk to its lowest ebb, not because they are still in love (desire a sexual relation with each other except as a last resort or to fulfill an obligation), but only because it is the lesser of two evils when divorce is considered worse. Now put on your thinking caps and follow me carefully, because the solution is marvelous to behold.

When a boy and girl reach an age where they desire to start dating (this is that time in life when the body unconsciously moves the mind in the direction of sex), they know there isn't a person in the world who would desire to make them fall in love and then break their heart by rejecting them, when it is also known in advance there will be no blame. Consequently, when a girl accepts her first date with a boy who appeals to her and then finds herself falling more and more in love whether it is returned or not (this is the key to the problem, which must be worked backwards to understand the solution), she is completely unafraid to confess her love and offer her body because she wants him for her husband and knows, just as certain as two plus two equals four, that he would never have taken her out unless the possibility existed of him falling in love with her. This is an undeniable fact because he knows that she would never hold him responsible for making her fall all the more in love with no intention of marrying her (staying with her), for possibly making her pregnant, and when it fully dawns on him that she must excuse everything he does, although he knows it would be his responsibility since nothing can make him hurt her this way unless he wants to, it becomes impossible for him to derive satisfaction from deflowering her under these conditions. He is compelled to do everything in his power to stay away from this kind of situation. Could you, with a clear conscience, allow a girl to fall in love enough to want you for her husband and then break her heart when you are absolutely certain that no one in the world, not even the girl to be so terribly hurt, would ever blame you because you know that she must turn the other cheek for satisfaction?

This means that when a boy discovers, through these undeniable relations, that a girl is perfectly willing to go the extreme once he has encouraged her to fall in love by kissing, petting, fooling around in general, he recognizes that there is no advantage, in fact, a complete waste of time, to pay flattering compliments and hand her a line when knowing that he will be compelled, of his own free will, to refuse her body when it is offered... unless he is serious with her, that is, unless he feels, from the very first time he sees her, that he could fall in love. This forces him to ask out (the girl could ask; it makes no difference under these conditions) only the kind of girl that appeals enough to become his wife and forces her to accept a date with only the kind of boy that appeals enough to become her husband. They have no other choice unless they prefer the risk of making people fall in love with them and then find it necessary to break their heart by leaving. If a boy should ask a girl for a date who doesn't desire him, she would simply turn him down because she knows where it might lead, but he could never be hurt by this initial refusal. However, this does not mean that they are forced to stay because to leave would be a hurt for which there would be no blame, as was already explained, but it does prevent them from considering sex as separate from dating. If they want sex, they are compelled to desire searching for the person with whom they feel they could fall in love. This prevents them from holding on a string of prospects for marriage just in case they can't find someone who is considered of greater value, which prevents the contest wherein there must be losers who get hurt. This means that when a boy or girl asks the other for a date, they are actually saying, in so many words, "Honey, you appeal to me very much from every point of view, and if you go out with me, I am going to accept this as an invitation to make love." And the other, if the date is accepted, answers in so many words, "Honey, I know what you want because I want it too." Consequently, when they are in a fond embrace and his hand begins to wander, instead of checking this motion, as a girl was often compelled to prefer because she didn't know if this was to her advantage, she only encourages him all the more, as he encourages her. Obviously, both of them will become very passionate and desire to go the extreme, but they will want this very much without the slightest fear that either will ever hurt the other by leaving, even though they can if they want to, but they won't want to. And the moment they indulge with or without contraception and regardless of what they do to satisfy each other, they are married, but not because they took out a license, not because they were pronounced man and wife by a priest or rabbi, but only because they will fall so much in love when nothing inhibits their sexual pleasure and they're prevented from striking a first blow that they will never desire another sexual partner. As to whether they are too young to have sex; are they too young to masturbate?

God created them with a built-in standard as to when they are ready. This has nothing to do with when they feel ready to raise a family. However, they are compelled to think like never before because they won't want to burden their parents with additional expenses when knowing there would be no blame; consequently, they would be extremely careful about pregnancy. But the enjoyment of a sexual relation, which will make them fall more and more in love, wouldn't cost their parents a dime. They will remain together, as you will soon have verified, not because to leave would break the other's heart, but primarily because they are in love and will remain in love.

In our present world, they can get married without having sexual intercourse and can have the latter without the former, but in the new world, it will be impossible to have one without the other because they are one and the same.

Boys and girls never gave much thought to the consequences of their actions because they were driven by a natural desire for sex, which is their birthright, and when somebody fell in love and got hurt, the answer was, "What am I supposed to do, marry the girl because we had sex? She knew what she was doing, and I didn't commit myself." By knowing that he would be blamed, he was always allowed to shift his responsibility, but he had no better choice because the pressure for a sexual relation was striking the first blow since marriage was out of the question at that young age. By removing all the blame, the pressure is also removed because he can have a sexual relation immediately, and there is no possibility for unrequited love to develop, no chance for any girl to be swept off her feet and lose her virginity out of wedlock, no chance for a double standard to make some girls bad and others good, no chance for a boy and girl to hurt each other in any way where sex is concerned because all the factors truly responsible are prevented from arising. Furthermore, once all the words are removed that now judge some people inferior physiognomic productions of the human race, everybody becomes perfectly equal in value except to the person making a choice: one face is not better looking than another, just different, although we will always find certain differences we like better. It is true that we have already been conditioned to move in the direction of certain differences, but we cannot be hurt when these differences reject us at the very outset, and when other differences will never be directly or indirectly criticized. If a boy desires a type of girl like Elizabeth Taylor who does not desire his type, he is compelled to put the proverbial horse before the cart and search for the type of girl who is ready to have sex with him. He will then fall in love with her sexual organs regardless of what her features are like, because nobody will ever refer indirectly to her as ugly by calling other types beautiful, which in our present world could possibly make him regret his choice and keep an eye out for someone who would be looked upon by others as having more to offer in the way of physical appearance. But how is it possible for him to regret his preference for a mate when they stop criticizing his choice and when he has fallen in love with her, which takes place after, not before, sexual intercourse? Adultery arises in most cases from the fact that a boy and girl have fallen out of love. When this is prevented, they will desire each other until death do they part. I will demonstrate this in a later chapter. For now, however, I shall reveal my final discovery, which will absolutely shock all mankind. It is not easy to follow the reasoning, but take your time and you will understand.

SEYMOUR LESSANS

CHAPTER SIX
OUR POSTERITY

EVEN THOUGH THE OTHER two discoveries will bring about an entirely new world for the benefit of all mankind (the blueprint of which will be demonstrated in the following chapters as I extend the principles into other human relations), the discovery to be revealed in this chapter is my favorite. When thoroughly understood, it might be yours, too.

Now tell me, wouldn't it make you feel wonderful to know, as a matter of undeniable knowledge, equivalent to two plus two equals four, that there is nothing to fear in death, not only because it is impossible to regret it but primarily because – don't jump to any hasty conclusion – you will be born again and again and again. I am not speaking of reincarnation or a spiritual world of souls or any other theory, but of the flesh, of a mind and body alive and conscious of existence as you are this moment. Are you smiling? Can't you see, once again, Eric Johnston refusing to listen because he was so certain man's will is free, or Nageli not investigating Mendel's discovery because the very core was regarded as impossible? Didn't many of you smile when first hearing that man does not have five senses? I expect you to be skeptical, but to deny my discovery after you have studied the relations, not before. We have been unable to see this hidden law because our reasoning prevented it. But before I get into the proof, and to help you understand it, answer this question.

Doesn't it seem strange that of all the millions of years the earth has been in existence, you, of all people, should be born at this time to see the wonders of this world and the inception of the Golden Age? Why weren't you born back in the days of Socrates, or why did you have to be born at this time instead of a thousand years hence?

You might reply, "I was born at this time because my mother met my father, fell in love, got married, and had four children. I am the third. My grandparents gave birth to my parents, and so on. Furthermore, I have seen many people die, and they never return as new babies or in any other form. Therefore, since I, too, must die, why should I be an exception and return?"

This is all very true, but your reasoning as to what actually happens after your death is an inference based upon your observations during your life. When you die, you cannot possibly have any more observations. In other words, your reasoning doesn't reveal a deeper truth. Does matter itself reveal atomic energy? Do the individual planets, moon, and sun reveal the solar system? Do individual people reveal the mankind system unless we find certain undeniable laws? Certainly, your grandparents gave birth to your parents, who gave birth to four children, but this tells us nothing about the law it is necessary to understand to know why there is nothing to fear in death and why we will be born again and again and again. At one time, man was afraid of thunder, thinking it was the wrath of God. Until he discovered the cause of an eclipse, he was afraid that something terrible was going to happen, and it became an ominous sign that was blamed for whatever evil followed. Such is the reason it seems strange to be alive at this moment with all the millions of years behind you, simply because you don't understand the truth. When it is thoroughly explained, the strangeness disappears, but I must proceed with undeniable relations and begin with this statement, which I shall prove.

The actual reason it isn't strange to me that you are alive at this moment and conscious of your existence with the earth as old as it is, is simply because there is no such thing as the past or future, only the present; consciousness, like the sun, can only exist in the present, and it is absolutely impossible for any consciousness to exist but our very own. It is we who will exist many years from now, not our posterity. But the fact that your consciousness is the only consciousness that can exist does not mean that other people are not conscious of their existence also, only that they cannot be seen except through our consciousness. It would therefore make no difference when the question is asked – "Doesn't it seem strange?" simply because we, our consciousness, will always be present to answer. Now pay close attention.

Since your body is no longer here when you die, who is the next child born? You can't say "him or her" because this observation must pass through your consciousness or mind, and you are no longer here since you just died, so who are we talking about? This means that since it is absolutely impossible to see this world except through your own consciousness (you must first be able to say "I" in order to say "him or her"), and since you are no longer here because you just died, this new child must be you, not the same individual, but someone who has gone through nine months of gestation, who will be given a name, inherit what was passed on to him, grow, recognize his own individuality, see the world in relation to himself, see people die who will never return, and see babies born who cannot possibly be himself because he is alive and conscious of his existence. Another way of saying the same thing is this: When I say "I," I must be talking about myself, and if everybody born must say "I," the chain is never broken, so no matter how often I die, no matter when the question is asked – "Doesn't it seem strange?" I or you will always be here to answer. However, let me clarify this in a different way.

Let us go back to the time just before you were conceived. We shall let A represent all the sperm pertaining to mankind, B all the ova, and the combination of one with the other will be C, which is you. Your parents have decided to create a child. This is you, but you don't know this yet, nor do they know whether you will be a boy or girl or what other characteristics you may have. You might be the first child, second, third, fourth, fifth, and so on. Now remember, you are not born yet, so you cannot possibly be conscious of your existence, but you are a potential candidate for this consciousness. However, as luck would have it, you die during your uterine journey when your mother has a miscarriage, which means that the conditions are exactly as they were before. But your mom and dad still want you, so they try again. This time, you are born only to die one month later of a heart attack after taking a look at your father. But still persistent and having a lot of fun, they try again with viable success, and here you are alive, conscious of your existence, and reading this book.

Now we shall assume for the purpose of clarity that 200 people comprise the total population on the earth, which means that upon your death, there were only 199. However, when you died, this body, this bubble of consciousness, is gone, which makes it impossible for you to say that the next child born is him or her because this relation must pass through your consciousness, and your consciousness is no longer here since you died. Therefore, since your family just lost you, which decreased the population to 199, and since these remaining 199 members are not you but still want you, number 200, the next infant born is not 201 but you, number 200, who will grow, develop, and become conscious of your existence. The conditions are exactly the same after your death as before your birth, and it is impossible for any child to be born who does not say "I". If you, the 200th member of your family, said "I" just before your death, and the remaining members of your family are still alive at the time that you died, and if it is impossible to be born and not say "I" because everything must be seen through your consciousness, then it cannot possibly be him or her, number 201, that is born, but you, number 200.

What is the actual difference between the potential you who died during the uterine journey, the you who died one month after birth, or the you who will die in a relatively short period of time? Because you are conscious of your individuality and existence during your lifetime, write a book, build a home, make a lot of friends who cry when you die doesn't take away from the fact that you are a combination of A and B, which continues in existence even while you are alive. If you had died a hundred thousand times in the uterus or otherwise, eventually you, which is a word to describe the consciousness of differences about yourself after your parents create you, would have been born. Consequently, the consciousness of your individuality, without understanding that you are not only C, the hereditary differences that die, but A and B, which never die because they are carried along from generation to generation and, when united, develop into your consciousness of existence, make you perceive an improper relation.

If you examine all the facts, you will find them undeniable. This I or ego that you feel is definitely a reality, for it is you, no one else, that tastes, sees, smells, touches, and hears. But this consciousness is not only an individual thing like the various differences about yourself, which we have considered C, but also A and B, the potential consciousness that exists in the germinal substance. Since this substance is that from which your ego, the feel of yourself as an individual, is composed, and since this I or ego is also the conscious expression of the germinal substance, both are one and the same. Consequently, the consciousness of all mankind is the ego or I of the germinal substance which imparts individuality upon the birth of a child as a tree does to a leaf in the spring of the year. But this all-pervasive consciousness (and here is the solution again) can only be your consciousness because it is impossible to see this universe through any body but your own. You must be on the inside looking out because it is impossible to be on the outside of your body and look at this universe, which means that you must be able to say "I". In other words, to draw up a comparison for a still better understanding, if we let A and B, that which is carried along from generation to generation, equal a huge, live, headless body that never dies, but from which human heads begin to grow, the first head will say – "I am the only human alive." When the second head appears, he will say – "I am alive and I see you, my Siamese brother, and we are the only two humans alive." When the third head appears, she says – "Our family consists of my two brothers and myself, and I am alive, conscious of my existence." If God chopped off one of these heads and, like a hydra, another one appeared instantly in its place, the new head would say – "I am alive, conscious of my existence, and there are only three heads in our family." This is exactly what happens when you die: your head is chopped off from the body of A and B, which continues in existence from generation to generation, and when a boy and girl mate, they create you, C, a body that grows and develops and says – "I am alive, conscious of my existence. I have brothers and sisters, a mother and father." But when you die, your body and consciousness are gone, only to be born again. Consequently, death is a mirage to those who die and a reality only to the living, and it is our ability to recognize these deeper relations that gives us our knowledge of personal immortality and our freedom from the fear of death. However, when someone dies, it is true he is gone and will never return to us because these relations are also undeniable. But the full realization of what death actually is will destroy the desire to preserve corpses in cemeteries, for this is only a waste of valuable land and the bodies of the dead. No one will deny that it is sad to lose a loved companion, but the satisfaction in preserving this unliving bit of matter can only be gotten when ignorance of the truth engenders the desire.

The perception of these relations makes it obvious that the same general experiences we have gone through of being little boys and girls with a mother and father, growing up and remarking about the time when we believed the earth flat, our will free, and our eyes a sense organ, will continue just as long as man is able to reproduce himself. In our Golden Age, the inception of which will take place shortly, we will raise our family in complete freedom from the evils that were compelled to come into existence during our years of development. We will live to a ripe old age without overpopulating the earth and die only to be born for the same happiness again and again and again.

Well, isn't this the most wonderful knowledge? However, I still have to demonstrate how it is now possible to permanently remove the "evils that were compelled to come into existence during our years of development," by continuing to extend the basic principle – Thou Shall Not Blame.

BEYOND THE FRAMEWORK OF MODERN THOUGHT

SEYMOUR LESSANS

CHAPTER SEVEN
THE FIRST BLOW

AT THIS JUNCTURE, IT is extremely important to understand that there are three forms to this first blow, and we have been discussing the second form only, which cannot be prevented until the first form, struck by the law of self-preservation, is permanently removed. Let me explain.

In Chapter Two, I wrote, "As before, you are trying to decide whether to hurt us in some way, but you have had everything removed from which you might have been able to justify your act. You simply see an opportunity to gain at our expense, but you will not be a loser if you decide against it. You are contemplating the first blow under changed conditions." In other words, the demonstration that followed assumed that all justification had been removed before our basic principle could prevent the desire to strike a first blow, which means that this could be a second or retaliatory blow, if not to strike it would make us a loser. Consequently, the first form of the first blow is the economic condition, beyond our personal control, that makes us a loser unless we do something to hurt others, but when this condition is permanently removed, there can be no retaliation to it, which means that the same act to hurt them that before was struck to prevent ourselves from becoming a loser could only be done to gain at their expense, making it the second form of first blow which can be prevented by our basic principle simply because not to strike it wouldn't make us a loser. However, since this is an extremely crucial point, I shall clarify it.

At this moment of time throughout the earth, everybody has attained a certain standard of living which can be measured in dollars and cents. It is the amount of money we consume from week to week on an average in order to maintain our particular way of life, but it does not include taxes, business or job expenses, insurance premiums, donations, or any money invested for the purpose of improving our standard. This means that if we were earning $300 a week, as an example, but were paying out $60 a week on taxes, $20 a week on job expenses, $35 a week on insurance premiums, $10 a week on donations, and $25 a week on investments, our standard of living would be $150 a week. We shall call this 100%. Now, if we, due to circumstances beyond our control, are forced to go below this 100%, then we become a loser, and the law of self-preservation, the constant fear that this could happen, compels us to do any number of things to prevent or recoup our loss. But when it becomes impossible for us to be hurt by going below this 100%, which removes the first form of first blow, then we cannot make matters worse for ourselves by not hurting others, which means that any hurt considered by us to them can be prevented by the basic principle because there is no way we can find greater satisfaction in gaining at their expense when we know they will never blame us. But let me explain this in another way.

Before our basic principle can prevent businesspeople from desiring to raise prices, the unions from striking for higher

wages, government from increasing taxes and going to war –
all for the purpose of improving their standard of living, that
is, of going over their 100% – we must prevent the possibility
that they are doing these things to keep from going below
their standard of living or 100%. When the unions discover
that inflation has eaten or could eat into their salaries, when
a businessman sees that his expenses have increased because
of rising labor costs, when rising prices eat into the salaries of
government workers, the choice is either to suffer this loss or
do something about it. If a government must choose between
a depression or war, the latter may be judged the lesser of two
evils. A salesman who needs a certain income to meet his
expenses doesn't hesitate to lie or cheat in order to make a
sale, simply because telling the truth might make him a loser.
In reality, if this condition or form of first blow is not
permanently removed, the basic principle would not only not
prevent this retaliation, it would make it impossible to turn the
other cheek for greater satisfaction. However, to accomplish
the removal of this economic condition without hurting or
blaming any country, individual or group for anything, which
rules out all existing governments because they cannot even
approach the problem without blame or hurt in some form, I
am going to demonstrate how it is now possible to guarantee
to all the people in the world who are doing, or able to do
something to earn a living, whether legal or illegal and while
decreasing taxes, ending inflation, war and crime (that is,
without robbing Peter to pay Paul), that should they ever find
themselves in a position of being laid off, displaced, unable
to get a job/business or one that pays enough to sustain the
standard of living attained at the start of the transition, but

only after using up all their reserve cash towards this end; and if there are some people who are below a basic standard and cannot find a job doing something to earn the necessaries of life, we will lend them, without interest, the materials or money needed. Then, when our basic principle is introduced as a permanent condition of the environment, it will be impossible for them to desire taking advantage of us in order to gain at our expense, simply because the justification (the possibility they could go below their standard of living) has been removed, although they will be completely free to take certain risks that could hurt us, if they want to. This does not mean they will be denied an opportunity to exert their initiative for the purpose of improving their standard of living (going over their 100%), but only that they will prefer finding ways and means of doing this without taking any risks that could hurt us because they know we must turn the other cheek for our satisfaction. It also means that they will desire to do everything in their power to sustain their own standard without having to borrow from us, simply because the realization that we would never blame them for taking advantage to get money that otherwise we could use to improve our own standard, denies their conscience the necessary satisfaction to consider this in any way. Should they deem it necessary to get financial help and then find a job or business which allows them to earn more than enough to sustain their standard of living, they would want to pay back what was lent to them before improving their standard. This does not mean that we are going to lend people money to stay in business, although we will help them maintain their standard if forced out and unable to help themselves. You will understand this much better as we proceed, so don't get discouraged or assume this is impossible. Just bear in mind that I cannot put everything down at one time.

The reason we do not include insurance premiums in estimating our guarantee is simply because these do not have anything to do with our standard of living. We hope we will never have to use this emergency coverage, but while we work, we can afford the premiums. When we lose our job or business and cannot sustain our standard of living, it is obvious that we must drop our policies. However, should an emergency arise during the time that we are borrowing money to sustain our standard, such as an accident, operation, fire, etc., we would be able to borrow the additional money since we are guaranteed against going below our 100%.

Now before I demonstrate how it is possible to make the guarantee work for the benefit of all mankind by extending it together with the basic principle into the economic world, it is important to understand that we have been striking the third form of first blow with impunity and in the name of justice by calling it a second or retaliatory blow. This occurs when we hurt people not because they did something to hurt us, which is the retaliatory blow that, when removed, prevents the desire to strike a first blow, but only because they did not do what we judged they should, and we blame them for our disappointment or their disobedience. A perfect example of this takes place when we fine them for going 40 miles an hour in a 25-mile zone. They did absolutely nothing to hurt us, but we justified this hurt to them by calling it punishment, which implies that they struck the first blow. However, if in fact this act was a first blow, then they could not have done it knowing that they would not be criticized, but the very fact that not blaming does not prevent them from doing it offers undeniable proof that our hurt to them, not their disobedience, is the first blow.

By our judging what they should do for us, which judgment cannot possibly be for the purpose of preventing a first blow because they would not desire to strike one under the changed conditions, we are actually trying to get them to do what they have a perfect right not to do, and then when they refuse to do it, we criticize, blame, or hurt them in some way. In other words, there is a conflict of desire here, but it should be obvious who has the right-of-way since to satisfy our desire, we need them, but to satisfy their desire not to do what we want them to do, they don't need us. However, I shall clarify this because it is an extremely crucial point.

When the truck driver approaches the intersection and sees that the light is still red, he decides to stop, not because we are telling him what to do but simply because the risk of hurting us and the knowledge that he would be responsible is so terrible to contemplate when we refuse to blame him for what he cannot excuse, that he is compelled to prefer stopping. But when he stops and sees that it is perfectly safe to cross even though the light is still red, he has just as much a right to do so as he had a right to cross without stopping. However, though the basic principle can prevent accidents because they are first blows, it can never prevent people from going 40 miles an hour in a 25-mile zone, from crossing on a red light, from drinking and driving, etc., if they think there is no risk involved, whereas we were hurting them because they didn't agree with our judgment (our laws, our commandments, our standards, etc.) of what was right for themselves. Therefore, the need to judge what is right for them becomes obsolete when we know that they will never hurt us, which means that to criticize, blame, or hurt them because they don't do what we tell them to do, becomes the third form of first blow that we cannot desire to strike when we know that they will never blame us. This proves conclusively that when others know what is a first blow, we don't have to tell them not to strike it because the basic principle prevents the desire, which means that they are completely free, their conscience clear, to do anything they judge is right for themselves without fear of criticism. For the very first time in the history of the human race, we are compelled, by the knowledge of our true nature, which reveals what is better for ourselves, to mind our own business, that is, to stop judging what is right for others. This, too (the third form of the first blow), you will understand much better as we proceed.

SEYMOUR LESSANS

CHAPTER EIGHT

THE DISPLACED AND THE GUARANTEE

IT SHOULD BE OBVIOUS that the transition to this new world must take place on a gradual basis because the government cannot remove from an individual the possibility of punishment as a necessary condition of the environment, until he receives his guarantee and passes an examination to prove that he understands what it means that man's will is not free, that is, understands the two-sided equation, what constitutes a fist blow, and who has the right-of-way when desires conflict. When this test has been passed and he signs a statement that he will never again blame another citizen of this Golden Age for anything, he himself becomes one by receiving an identification number which is placed on a card to be worn on the outside, and on tags for his car. There can be no punishment should he break this agreement and not turn the other cheek, but how is it possible for him to break this or any agreement when he knows there will be no blame for striking this first blow. However, in order for him not to be blamed by his government, and in order for his government not to be blamed by the governments of other nations, the political and military leaders of the world must become our first citizens.

This will allow the transition to get underway without the possibility of further wars because the very people who have the power to start one will be stopped by the guarantee, which denies them any justification, and by their realization that there will be no retaliation by those who must turn the other cheek for their satisfaction. This means that our next citizens will be the police, who will be displaced in proportion as the noncitizens decrease; the armed forces; the manufacturers of war equipment, lawyers; the unions, and all the others who know their manner of earning a living is coming to an end. This will include private eyes, floor walkers, people who sell liability insurance, credit investigating and collection agencies, and all those schools, religious or otherwise, that have been teaching us how to cope with a hostile environment that will no longer be. How is it possible to continue paying a religious organization to show us the way when God has delivered us from evil? How is it possible to spend on learning the art of war and self-defense when no one will ever again attack us? We can continue to spend in this direction if we want to, just as a businessman can continue to hire floor walkers, but how is it possible to want to when this serves no purpose, and the money could be used to improve our standard of living?

Millions upon millions upon millions of people will be permanently displaced from their manner of earning a living, while millions more will find their income dropping, but not only without being hurt because they can borrow what is needed to sustain their standard of living, but without causing others to be hurt. However, they will not prefer to quit their job because this is a voluntary move and does not entitle them to receive the guarantee, which means that they must be released by their employer and consume all their reserve cash before coming to us for financial help. If they are in business for themselves and their services or products have come to an end, such as with war equipment, they are free to look immediately for something else. But if what they are selling has not been permanently displaced, although the buyers have decreased, they will prefer to remain at what they are doing as long as this requires them to borrow less from the guarantee to sustain their standard of living. If they reach a point whereby changing businesses or jobs they would need to borrow less or nothing at all from the guarantee, then their conscience will allow them to make a change. However, should they wish to gamble part of their standard of living in order to make a change before they need our financial help, this is their business, but if they fail to succeed and then require our help, they must be satisfied with the new standard of living they imposed on themselves, since what lowered their standard was not beyond their control. I shall elaborate more on this shortly.

It is humorous to observe that although we must enter this new world of our own free will because no force will be used, the comparison of what we now have with what will be gives us no choice because our will is not free to move against what gives us greater satisfaction, which forces us to desire studying for the examination so we can become citizens as quickly as possible after the transition has been officially launched.

Many laws are in existence that do not represent first blows while denying an opportunity to improve our standard of living unless we take the risk of their violation. As an example, in many cities of the United States, poolroom proprietors are denied an opportunity to stay open longer if they want to, as with other businesses, while certain forms of gambling are considered illegal. Can any person in the world make us place a bet unless we want to? This means that citizens will have opportunities to improve their standard of living the very moment the laws that deny this no longer apply to them.

Because our experts have never known how to put an end to all the hurt in human relations, although many of them thought they did, they blamed the theft of a car on the person who left his keys in the ignition, murder and robbery on the sale of guns, sex crimes on pornography and the lack of strict censorship, and our children not developing as we hoped on nightclubs, gambling houses, brothels, and other dens of iniquity. However, this does not mean that when the laws are removed, these things will flourish. On the contrary, prostitution, the sale of guns, alcoholism, drug addiction, and many other things will come to an end because there will be less and less buyers to keep the sellers in business, not because these things are first blows. How can a drug pusher make a living when citizens can sell the same thing at a cheaper price? The drug store is loaded with poisons we can take into our body if it gives us satisfaction to do so, and if we want to dive off the Empire State building to see if we can make a three-point landing on our head without killing ourselves, this is our business. In other words, we are not only not going to blame you for any hurt you do to us, but not blame you for any hurt you choose to risk doing to yourself. But though the words legal, illegal, lawful, and unlawful become obsolete for citizens, noncitizens will continue to come under the laws of their nation until they pass the examination.

This means that a citizen, with the exception of those who will still represent the laws of their government, will be forced to act toward noncitizens as if they are already citizens, that is, never strike them with a first blow even though he knows they would blame him, simply because he knows the government will not blame him for anything he does, which denies him greater satisfaction in striking this blow when the people who are protecting noncitizens during the transition must turn the other cheek. This forces him to drive his car as if there are no noncitizens and allows him to drop his liability insurance because the laws to make him liable have become obsolete for him. However, should an accident occur between him and noncitizens, he could still sue or bring charges against them because this is not a first blow if he feels that he had the right-of-way, and the same thing applies should an accident occur between noncitizens because they are still living in the old world. But if he feels they had the right-of-way in an accident involving him, his guilt will be overwhelming because the laws will not hold him responsible. Even the need for deductible insurance will decrease proportionately as the citizens increase. What are the risks that something unforeseen will damage our cars when everybody stops doing those things that cause accidents?

It is humorous to observe that if a motor vehicle operator wants to speed, go through red lights, stop signs, or do any number of things that risk hurting others without the police being on his back, or if someone wants to steal without the possibility of going to prison, all he has to do is become a citizen and he will be completely free of the laws. But when he does become one, he will be compelled by a superior law and the guarantee to sacrifice any such desires as that alternative which is better for himself. This proves conclusively that just as soon as science confirms this work as an undeniable blueprint of a world that must come to pass out of absolute necessity when our political and military leaders understand the principles, the inception of this Golden Age can officially begin. The transition will be completed when prisoners, the last ones to take the test, have passed the examination.

TAXES AND
FINANCING THE GUARANTEE

Since raising prices and striking for higher wages are first blows which we cannot desire to strike after becoming citizens and receiving our guarantee, and since this blow, no matter where it originates in our present world, is the source of inflation, we must enact an international law during the transition that will punish severely any noncitizens who choose to violate it. But remember, if this law annoys them, all they have to do is become citizens, and they will be completely free to strike this blow to their hearts' content.

Now it is important to understand that we, as citizens, can no longer be told that we must pay taxes or else suffer the consequences, which means that the forceful collection of taxes and the filling out of forms to check on our honesty have come to an end. However, not to pay taxes at all is a first blow when our income is above the standard of living recorded as our guarantee, which means that once we are satisfied that our tax share cannot be more equitable, our desire to contribute this amount is controlled by two factors. One, is our realization that the guarantee removes the need for any citizen to hurt us in order to prevent himself from going below his standard of living or from being without the necessaries of life. Two, is our realization that we have it in our power to force other citizens to pay our share without their knowledge (you will be shown this shortly), which means that we would be gaining at their expense. But when we fully realize that they would not blame us even if they knew, it becomes impossible for us to find greater satisfaction in not contributing our share. This new method of contribution, not taxation, will displace the Bureau of Internal Revenue and everybody connected with the collection of taxes, but only in proportion as the citizens increase. So once again, pay close attention.

Since to increase taxes in any way, shape, or form is a first blow, as is raising prices and striking for higher wages, taxes will never be increased, only decreased, and the percentages we were paying when noncitizens will continue as a guide. Therefore, since no one henceforth will ever again collect our taxes, it should be obvious that the next step is to keep our own quarterly record of the total amount of money we would have paid the government had it been collected for us. In other words, if our employer was withholding $650 for the quarter, which includes state, city, and social security taxes, he would pay us our gross income each week, and we would deduct our expenses for the quarter because there will be no refunds (let us say as an example $150), and then record $500. If our property taxes for the year are $840, we would simply record one-fourth, or $210, for the quarter. The seller will see that we are citizens by our identification card and will not include any sales tax, but will list it on our receipt for our record. If we spent $800 for a 3-month period and the sales tax was 4%, we would record $32 plus any other excise taxes. This same procedure applies to corporations and includes every form of tax, fee, or license paid to the government.

Now at the end of a quarter we are going to need money to finance the guarantee, but this is very simply solved because a governor will know through his accounting department how much is required in his state for that quarter, and all the governors will submit their figure to the office that computes the total for the nation; and if there are any nations that cannot meet their own guarantee after consuming all their reserve cash, the amount needed would be submitted to the office that computes the total for the world.

Now we shall assume that after everybody got displaced whose manner of earning a living was not needed any longer, and allowing for many of these and other people using their reserve cash to finance themselves while looking for new employment, it was estimated that 20% of the total taxes recorded for the quarter would be needed to support the guarantee, which means that an announcement of 20% would be made to all taxpayers throughout the earth, and if our quarterly total was $100, $200, $300, $400, $1000, $2000, $3000, $4000, etc., we would remit 20% of our total. However, this first announcement must be an estimate, which means that it could be over or under the total amount required. Therefore, when the quarterly amount is received and totaled up, we would know immediately that 80% remains, and if we were short, we would know exactly what additional percent to ask for in the second announcement. If we were over, it would be held in reserve for the next quarter. As for the remaining services of government, such as the Sanitation Department, the

Traffic Division, Road Maintenance, Public Schools, etc., these would be paid for in the same manner but on a local level.

Each department will have its own budget, and when the first announcement is made, let us say of 2% for the schools, 2% for road maintenance and the traffic division, 1% for garbage collection, 1% for the Fire Department, etc., we would remit the total of these percentages; let us say it was 8% of the same total gathered together for the quarter. But if we do not have a car or children in public school, we would not send in that particular percent asked for, and this applies to any program that we do not desire to participate in. However, this does not stop those who have ideas from getting their own financing, but this has nothing whatever to do with those remaining services of government or the guarantee. If a group of scientists wish to land men on the moon again, this is their business, but the money to pay for it is our business. They might be able to raise enough on a closed-circuit TV show by selling tickets in advance, but however they raise this money, it cannot be done by force. Now, once the second announcement is made to let us know, one way or the other, whether more or no more is needed, the remaining money in our possession for that quarter becomes a tax profit, which we can spend or invest as each of us desires.

This system cannot be more equitable. It doesn't blame us for anything, doesn't tell us what must be done or else, and if we don't want to send in our share, this is our business, but we will know that what we don't pay will be picked up by the rest of the taxpayers on the second announcement, which means that we would be gaining at the expense of those who would not blame us even if they knew. Move in this direction if it is possible to derive greater satisfaction, especially when you know that should you ever need money to sustain your own standard of living, we would not hesitate to lend it. Now let me show you some of the most fantastic changes that must come about for the benefit of all mankind as a result of the guarantee and basic principle.

As those displaced individuals with reserve cash are forced to spend their money on supporting themselves until it runs out or they find another job or business; as each government is forced to use all its reserve cash to finance the displaced who cannot find work and do not have money of their own; and as the non-displaced will desire to spend or invest all their reserve cash to improve their standard of living because the need to save for a rainy day has been rendered obsolete by the guarantee, billions upon billions upon billions of dollars (perhaps trillions throughout the earth) will be forced into circulation and start a beneficious cycle (the exact opposite of the vicious cycle known as inflation) by creating an ever increasing demand for the labor of those people without jobs. Little by little by little, as the displaced find work which increases our tax profit, the money needed to finance the guarantee becomes less and less and less, while the money to spend or invest on improving our standard of living becomes more and more and more.

The very moment someone becomes a citizen, he will pay his taxes in the manner just described, but the government will only make an announcement if the money already in its possession and received from noncitizens is inadequate. In other words, if the government has enough cash reserve to cover its expenses for the first quarter, which includes the guarantee, citizens will be told that what they recorded for the quarter is a total profit. Now observe next how the money to improve our standard of living increases still more by the fact that prices are forced to come down.

Since money lenders can no longer discriminate against any citizen who comes to them for a loan simply because they know he has impeccable credit under the changed conditions since not to pay it back in accordance with the terms agreed upon would be a hurt for which he knows he would never be criticized, he needn't pay higher rates of interest to the small loan companies and higher prices to the installment houses, simply because he can borrow and buy at the source that charges the least. As a consequence, since these small loan companies and installment houses must do everything in their power to sustain their own standard of living before coming to us for help, they are given no choice but to lower their interest and prices in order to compete with the department stores, discount houses, and the banks. But if after reducing their prices and interest they are forced to go below their standard of living, their conscience would still not allow them to get out of the business they're in as long as by reducing their interest and prices still more, they would hurt us less. In other words, if someone in business with a standard of living of $500 a week has discovered that he is $200 short of the mark, he can borrow this amount from the guarantee, but if he cannot find a new job or business that pays more than $300 towards his guarantee of $500, he would be forced to stay where he is because the money we would have to lend him would be less. And even if this means that he must reduce his prices ridiculously low to meet his own standard of living and lessen the amount he needs to borrow from us, this is what he must do to avoid hurting those who will never blame him. Let me explain this another way.

Supposing a television repairman in business for himself has discovered that he cannot earn enough to meet his standard of living. Since he cannot increase prices to solve his problem, he must lower prices. This will cause his competitors to lose business and lower prices to maintain their standard of living. On the other hand, even if he is having no problem maintaining his standard of living but would like to improve it, since he can never raise prices, he is compelled to lower prices and sell in volume which forces his competitors to do the same thing. This means that just as long as there are enough people to buy what he is selling so that he can still earn more and borrow less from us than if he changed his job or business, he is forced to remain at what he's doing unless he is willing to risk the possibility of reducing his own standard of living. In other words, if he is borrowing from us $200 a week to maintain his $500 standard but sees an opportunity to earn $600 to a thousand a week by changing jobs, this is his business and his gamble, but if he should fail and therefore need help from us, the most he would be entitled to is the $200 we were lending him before he made his change. The risk is his because this is something he is doing to himself, not something beyond his control. He could cheat us if he wants to because we are not going to check on his honesty, but he cannot find greater satisfaction in doing this when he knows that we would never blame him even if we knew. Should this be done, however, and reported to us, we would investigate without blame, just as we would investigate why a citizen is not paying back his creditor in accordance with the terms agreed upon. The very fact that the investigation would only reveal to the citizen doing this that we must turn the other cheek prevents him from doing anything that might cause an investigation. But the investigation is necessary just in case someone becomes mentally incapable of continued control by the guarantee and the principles of the examination. Should this be the case, his family would have to assume responsibility for him, but no one would blame or punish him in any way, even if it was necessary to confine him to an institution for treatment. But mental illness, in the new world, will be virtually wiped from the face of the earth.

OTHER CHANGES

All the people who are receiving unemployment compensation or welfare have a decision to make. They can continue to get the same amount, not as a loan, as long as they are unable to find work, but once they find employment, the amount they were receiving then becomes their guarantee, which means that should they ever lose that job and need our help because they cannot finance themselves or locate another job, they can borrow the money that was originally given to them as long as necessary. However, if they prefer to estimate their standard of living from the first job they get after they become citizens, then they will be placed immediately under the guarantee and be forced to use up all their reserve cash to finance themselves before continuing to receive the same assistance. Should they not have any reserve cash and not be able to find employment, we will lend them the same amount they were receiving. But once they find a job and estimate their standard of living therefrom, that figure will be the one guaranteed should they ever need our assistance, although they will never be able to improve their standard until they first pay back what was borrowed. This also applies to those people who are already retired when the transition begins. Correction: This does not apply to retired people. You must bear in mind that mistakes can be made in extending the principles, but this does not in any way affect the principles. This kind of mistake is equivalent to one a teacher might make when telling his students that traveling in a car at the speed of 50 mph, you would reach a destination of 250 miles in five hours and ten minutes. If he was corrected and saw his mistake, he would just acknowledge it as I just did. There might be other similar mistakes, but they are of no consequence because every extension can be tested and proven in an undeniable manner.

After it is launched, a person can retire according to the age and income specified by his country without borrowing the money to do so, simply because this is a voluntary move unless he is unable to work any longer. Should he decide to continue working after reaching a retirement age because his employer and conscience find his work satisfactory, this is his business, which means that if he does this until he becomes permanently unable to handle any kind of job, he would then come under his original guarantee, which is affected by his children shifting for themselves. Should he owe us money when he finally dies, we would simply wipe it off the books. Should he retire voluntarily at the specified age and receive the income that doesn't have to be paid back, he can add to this by finding work he can handle. However, when he cannot even handle this any longer, he would just receive money from his retirement plan.

What he chooses to do when he reaches a retirement age is his business.

Should a breadwinner lose his job or be laid off after his children have shifted for themselves and need to borrow money from us, his standard of living would be his original guarantee, less his expenses to support them. Should he die, so does his standard of living, but his wife, if not working, unable to find a job, without any cash reserve, and unable to meet her needs, can come to us for financial assistance. This is a loan, however, and we will continue to help her as long as necessary, but she will be under constant pressure to find some kind of employment or a new husband because her conscience will not allow her to increase the cost of the guarantee if she feels able to work. When she locates a job, her standard of living will be derived from it and be her guarantee thereafter. If this income does not allow her to meet her previous bills, we will still lend her the difference as long as necessary. If it does, and she has money left over with which to improve her standard of living, she must first pay back what was borrowed. This means that life insurance takes on an altogether different meaning.

Men were worried that their death might cause undue hardship for their families, but this becomes impossible under the guarantee. However, if someone wishes to invest part of his income on life insurance so that his wife will not have to go to work after his death, this is his business. But remember, the total amount of money she receives must be used on a weekly basis to meet her current needs because we will lend her the same amount when it runs out. She may be left enough so that she will never have to look for a job, but this money cannot be used to improve her standard of living unless it can be done without making it necessary to come to us for financial help.

All citizens will know that the money to finance the guarantee must come only from those of us who are in a position to improve our standard of living from this same money if it was not needed, which means that if they take advantage of the guarantee (borrow money they know they are not entitled to), they would know they are depriving us of using what we would prefer spending on ourselves. But when they fully realize that this would be a hurt to the very people who are guaranteeing that they will never go below their standard of living and never blame them, regardless of what they do, their conscience would deny them from moving in this direction for greater satisfaction. Consequently, they would be perfectly willing to have someone in the office where they are applying for their guarantee, if they are the least bit doubtful of what they're doing, to show them whether or not they are taking advantage. This means, as an example, that if a displaced person has a standard of living of $200 per week, $50 from an investment, and $150 from a job, but has $800 in reserve cash (non-invested money that has nothing to do with the $50 a week and could be used to improve his standard of living if he was not displaced), then this money becomes the source of his $150 a week until he consumes it or finds a new job. To use this money for any other purpose takes advantage of the guarantee, which means that before he can spend or invest it with a clear conscience to improve his standard of living, he must find a job that pays at least $150 a week. If he can only find one that pays less than this amount and still has reserve cash, he has two choices: either to reduce his standard of living to the new income, which then releases his reserve cash, to spend or invest as he pleases, or else to retain his standard of living and borrow the difference from his reserve cash until it runs out, at which time he can borrow from us. It should be obvious that what a person chooses to do is determined by the amount of his reserve cash, his standard of living, and how much less the new job pays. If it pays $145 a week when his standard of living is $150 and he has $25,000 in reserve or non-invested money, he might not wish to tie it up to supply himself with the $5 a week; consequently, he could set his new standard at $145 a week and release this money with a clear conscience. But when it is all used up, one way or another, and he should get laid off or displaced, his guarantee is then $145. By the same reasoning, the $50 a week from his investment is also guaranteed. If something should happen to cause him to earn less than this in dividends, and he has no cash reserve, he can borrow the difference, but if he chooses to reinvest or spend a portion of the principal from which is derived this $50 a week, then he again chooses to lower the amount we were guaranteeing. This also applies to someone who chooses to work less hours to earn less than his standard of living. If he was putting in 40 hours to earn $150 (this is the net amount of his standard of living), and then got a new job putting in the same amount of hours to earn the same amount of money, then he is meeting his guarantee; but if he decides to earn less by working 30 hours, this is his business, only he is not entitled to borrow the difference from the guarantee because this is a voluntary move, not something that was forced upon him or beyond his control.

If he feels that his reserve cash will run out before he finds a job, then he is under pressure to do everything in his power to locate one before it does; otherwise, he would be taking advantage of the guarantee. He must also go in the direction of what covers his guarantee regardless of the type of work available, not in the direction of what is easier to do; otherwise, if he chooses what pays less because it is easier, when what pays more, though harder, is available, then he chooses to lower his standard of living accordingly, unless he prefers to take advantage of the guarantee at our expense, for which he knows he will never be blamed. Even employers are prevented from taking advantage. If they paid him less, when the particular job calls for more, because they know he can borrow the difference, they would be gaining at his and our expense which they cannot find satisfaction in doing under the new conditions. But if the new job requires a certain amount of training and they find that he is not entitled to the full salary during this period, then the difference would be supplied by him if he has the reserve cash or borrowed from us. If his guarantee is $150, and his salary at the end of the training period $300 per week, while it was $100 during this time for 13 weeks which means that he borrowed from us $650 assuming that he had no reserve cash, then he would be obligated to pay back this amount at the rate of $150 a week at the end of his training period. But once he has paid back the money he borrowed, then he would be in a position to help finance the guarantee and share the other expenses of government he uses.

It shouldn't be necessary to relate all the changes (there are so many) that are compelled to come about in the economic world, simply because we can only go in a direction that will hurt no one. However, it is very important to understand, just in the event this was not made clear, that we are guaranteeing the standard of living derived from the particular job or business a person has when becoming a citizen. This means that if any individual quits his job, sells his business, changes his investment, or leaves his country to take other employment, this is a voluntary move unless he is forced to do so in order to borrow less from us. This prevents him from gambling at our expense, although he can if he wants to risk the possibility of lowering his own standard of living, because should he get laid off or displaced from his new job, he will have to settle for the basic standard until he can find other work. The great humor here is that the very people who want to leave communist countries will lose their desire when they become citizens, because they will not be subjected to the laws any longer and will want to continue receiving their guarantee.

The people in a communist nation will also go through the same procedure to become citizens and receive their guarantee, but the leaders will have no choice but to design a system that will allow all the people to receive an equal share of the profits regardless of what they do to earn a living, to benefit from their own initiative regardless of what is done with their extra time, and to improve their standard of living in any direction they wish to go because nothing will be done at the expense of others. However, no problems can arise because the guarantee and basic principle will be an undeniable standard to guide the people and their leaders as to the direction they are permitted to go by their conscience, which makes it unnecessary for me to show them that 3 is to 6 what 4 is to 8 when they can figure this out for themselves.

Mankind the world over, for the very first time, will be completely free to do what they think is better for themselves without fear of criticism or punishment, but they will never think it better to hurt others under the changed conditions. If a Black and White want to marry, this is their business. But in our present world, the critics have made it unbearable for many, but when the critic realizes that his criticism is striking a first blow for which we will never blame him, he can only find greater satisfaction in minding his own business, and this applies to any form of criticism. This means that the professional critic will be completely displaced, just as all beauty contests will be. How is it possible to have such a contest when each person's physiognomy is exactly equal in value except to certain individuals, and how is it possible to use their desire as a standard to judge that what they like less is an inferior production of the human race, unless words like beautiful and ugly make it appear that certain differences are of greater value intrinsically?

CHAPTER NINE
THE MEDICAL PROFESSION

THERE EXISTS A FORM of hurt different than any other in that it is done by us to ourselves when our fear that we will only get worse, or at least not better unless something is done immediately, compels us to consult doctors who, in their effort to earn a living by selling their services, convince us that they are fully capable of handling our problem but instead make us worse. It would make no difference what type of employer we are; if mistakes are made by those we hire, how is it possible to blame them when they could never have hurt us had we not employed them? It is true that we may have gotten hurt still more had they not been employed, but in either case, this is our responsibility, which reveals another great fallacy and form of injustice that exists today. We ask doctors to help us but force them to carry malpractice insurance just in case we are not satisfied with the results. Now, how is it possible for them to stay in business so they can help us when we need them if we do not wish to accept the responsibility of the risks involved? By imposing the need to carry this insurance, which blames them in advance for the risks they must take to earn a living and make us well, they cannot help but react with resentment towards us because there is no way they can offer

100% guarantees. This is somewhat equivalent to a mother who cannot swim offering money to bystanders if they would jump in and save her son from drowning and then blaming them for his death because they declined the offer or were unsuccessful in their effort. There is no way doctors can be held responsible for our getting worse or dying, and the fact that we do blame them only reveals once again how utterly confused we are. But observe a fantastic change that is compelled to come about out of absolute necessity.

When doctors become citizens, receive a guarantee that their standard of living will never go down, and know for a fact that they will never again be blamed no matter what happens, allowing them to drop their malpractice insurance and increase their net income, they are compelled to move in a different direction for greater satisfaction. In our present world, it is necessary for them to convince us that they can handle our problem; otherwise, we would not employ them and they would not get paid for their services. But under the changed conditions, they do not have to convince us, only themselves, that they know what they're doing, and if, in their professional opinion, there is the slightest doubt that their treatment might make matters worse for which they know there would be no blame, their only justification to take this risk since they cannot be financially hurt or blamed for refusing to take on the job is when it appears to them that we would be worse off if they prescribed nothing. For the very first time, by refusing to question their qualifications or hold them responsible for our mistake in hiring them, they are compelled to hold themselves responsible for hurting us unless they can convince themselves that our getting worse or dying was not because of anything they did. This means that if they have to choose between two risks: to prescribe something, even if this means advising us to leave the body completely alone to handle its own problem, or to tell us that they really are uncertain of what to do and therefore will not take on the job, they are forced to move in the latter direction because there is no way it is possible to blame themselves for not knowing what to do, whereas if we should get worse because they advised us, which implies they do know what they're doing, it becomes impossible not to blame themselves when we will never hold them responsible while guaranteeing their standard of living. This gives them no choice but to prescribe something only when they have convinced themselves that to do otherwise is definitely worse for us, which means that they would have to possess a fantastic amount of genuine knowledge. They would have to know all the side, distant, and accumulative effects of drugs to make certain that in correcting one problem, they do not create others still worse. They would have to know all the complications that could arise from an operation, whether it be from the anesthesia or the removal of certain parts of our body. If someone should die during an appendectomy, tonsillectomy, or from other surgery, the only way it is possible to clear their conscience of responsibility is to know that the patient would have been worse off without the operation, but they must convince themselves of this. They can no longer use the theory that our tonsils and appendix are vestigial organs to justify the operation, unless they can convince themselves that we are better off without these parts of our body. A young girl just recently had brain damage and died a few days later from the general anesthesia used to extract a wisdom tooth. Now, how does a dentist in the new world convince himself that he was not responsible for her death when no one blames him, and he knows there was a risk in using general anesthesia, especially? How is it possible for him to justify her death? If she was in pain and needed this tooth removed, why did he choose a general anesthetic without knowing whether she was allergic to the drug itself or when combined with other drugs already in her system? It is obvious that he prescribed this anesthetic without knowing these things. But how is it possible for him to face the parents of this girl to tell them of her death when they will simply break down in tears and not blame him in any way for what he knows they must excuse because they hired him, while he also knows there is no way he can ever shift his responsibility unless he can convince himself that the use of this general anesthesia and the operation itself was the lesser of two evils? If he cannot, he is forced to go through life with the death of this girl on his conscience. Now why should doctors take these risks when it is no longer necessary for the purpose of earning a living, unless they can actually see that these risks are the lesser of two evils? As a consequence, approximately 75% of what is prescribed today will be stopped by the doctors themselves, which means that approximately 25% of the hospitals, doctors, and nurses that are now in existence will suffice for our needs in the new world. The guarantee and basic principle will force doctors to become like Socrates, who was proclaimed the wisest man of his time for discovering that one of the differences between himself and other men was that he knew he didn't know the truth, whereas they didn't know either but thought they did. The doctors will simply tell us in the majority of cases when we consult them,

"I do not know what is better, to leave the body alone to heal itself or to prescribe something; therefore, I cannot take on the job of treating your problem."

In his book already quoted from, Durant writes, "In the first three months we were guilty of a grave blunder, for we allowed our child to be used as a laboratory for a new form of desiccated milk. It is a crime which many years of parental solicitude cannot quite clear from our memories. We believe now, with Ben Franklin, that the human race should beware of young doctors and old barbers." He blamed himself first for this grave blunder, but then shifted his responsibility to this young doctor. Under the changed conditions, however, should a mother not wish to use her breasts, for one reason or another which is her business, she will have to make the decision to take whatever risks there might be in the use of available formulas because the only time a doctor will suggest them is when her breasts are not functioning and any formula is better than starvation. How can a doctor possibly know that the formula might not cause severe colic, cramps, diarrhea, and so forth, when every child is different to a degree, and how is he going to feel when something happens, and he can blame nobody but himself? Why should he take the risk? There is no reason which forces a mother to choose between using the milk developed with and specifically for her baby or to play doctor herself. Now what choice does she have when the fear of certain risks gives her less, not greater, satisfaction?

SEYMOUR LESSANS

PART FOUR
THE DECLINE AND FALL OF THE REMAINING
EVILS
CHAPTER TEN – UNTIL DEATH DO THEY PART
CHAPTER ELEVEN – PARENTS AND CHILDREN
CHAPTER TWELVE – TEACHERS AND STUDENTS

BEYOND THE FRAMEWORK OF MODERN THOUGHT

CHAPTER TEN
UNTIL DEATH DO THEY PART

WHEN A BOY AND GIRL have sexual intercourse for the first time under the changed conditions as described in Chapter Five, they will fall more and more in love, not only because this passionate thrill of orgasmic ecstasy is a new experience that has become associated with one particular person, but also because they will never do anything to make the other fall out of love. They will remain together until death do they part, not because to leave would be a hurt for which there would be no blame, but only because they will know who has the right-of-way when desires conflict and will never strike a first blow. Let me show you exactly what I mean.

The problem begins when we do not know that an undeniable standard exists by which we can judge whether or not our own desires have the right-of-way when in apparent conflict with those of our partners, which allows us to use fallacious standards such as are contained in customs, laws, conventions, morals, and so forth, to justify hurting them to satisfy our genuine selfishness. But when we know who has the right-of-way, there is no problem. This means, as a perfect example, that if, after making love, our partners wish to sleep alone, which does not tell us what to do, this desire has the right-of-way over the desire to sleep together, simply because the desire to sleep together is a judgment of what is right for them. There is nothing wrong in desiring to sleep together, but it cannot be satisfied unless they want the same thing. If they do not desire to move to another bed after making love, then it is obvious that they, too, prefer to sleep together, but if they want to sleep alone while we do not, we are the selfish ones. In our present world, we justified criticizing them for wanting to sleep alone by invoking sleeping together as a condition of marriage. We expected them to show their love by sacrificing their desire in favor of ours, which only revealed our selfishness in expecting them to give up what they had the right-of-way not to. Then, when they still insisted on sleeping alone, and because we believed we were right, we called them selfish and struck the third form of first blow to get even for what they had the right-of-way to do. But when we know they have the right-of-way and that they would never blame us for striking this blow, no matter what we did to hurt them for not satisfying our desire, then we are given no choice but to sacrifice our selfishness and respect desires that make no demands on us. Reread chapter seven if you are still confused.

We have been blaming people for wearing a hat in our home as a sign of disrespect, not realizing that we were the ones disrespectful. To satisfy our desire, it is necessary to tell them what to do, but to satisfy their desire, they don't have to tell us to do anything. However, if wearing their hat in a theater blocked our view of the screen, they would want to remove it because this would be a first blow for which we would never blame them. Should they forget, they would want to be reminded because they could not get satisfaction in making us move to another seat when knowing that we must excuse what they can never justify. But if we ask them to leave our home unless they remove their hat, which is hurting no one, our realization that they would leave and not blame us for striking this first blow prevents us from using this or any other fallacious standard that heretofore allowed us to judge what was right for them.

With sexual intercourse, we have a slightly different problem because this is something we cannot do alone, yet to tell our partners that we are in the mood and expect them to honor our desire, or to touch them in any way for that purpose, takes for granted that they also want to make love or be fondled at that moment of time. Since this is an act of selfishness because it is a judgment of what we expect them to do for us unless they also desire this relation, we cannot touch them in any way until they extend us an invitation. But in our present world, should they reject us, we strike the third form of first blow by using the fallacious standard of justification that it is their marital obligation to have sex when we desire it so that they do not hurt us by neglecting our needs, which has forced many partners to make love when not in the mood as the lesser of two evils. However, it is true that if we do not satisfy our sexual needs, we are hurt, but since we cannot obligate our partners to do what they might not want to do and cannot judge what is right for them, the solution to this apparent impasse is for us to arouse their desire to want the same thing we want. Since we cannot make any physical contact because we do not know if this is what they want at that moment, we have no choice but to do everything in our power, one way or another, to arouse their desire to accept our invitation to make love without touching them in any way, which gives them the right to make physical contact with us if they want to. This means that we must assume responsibility for their lack of desire. In almost 100% of the times, because there will be no arguments or criticism, and we will learn every trick of the trade to stimulate desire without making physical contact, they will be sufficiently aroused to accept this invitation. However, if we still fail to arouse their desire after doing everything in our power, then it is true that we must wait for them to extend us an invitation but not for long because the normal desire for a sexual relation will have its way, and when they realize that even though we are hurt by not being able to satisfy our sexual needs, we would still never deprive them of the same by having a relation with another partner, their desire to satisfy our sexual needs will be aroused to the highest degree, as will our desire to satisfy them, but without one ounce of obligation.

The expression "for better or for worse," when interpreted properly, is absolutely true in the new world because we are never going to blame, but in our present environment, it allows us to strike the third form of first blow, making it worse for our partners, and excuse it by saying – "You married me for better or for worse." We can let ourselves get out of that shape that originally attracted them, and then when their desire to make love diminishes because we are less appealing, we blame them for what is our responsibility. But knowing they will never blame us for letting ourselves get out of that shape that originally attracted them, we are forced to do everything in our power to make their sexual life better because they will never hold us responsible for making it worse. The very fact that we are prevented from taking our partners for granted and must arouse their desire to accept an invitation each and every time we are in the mood to make love, will cause the greatest amount of passion imaginable. The honeymoon will never be over because we will keep ourselves fit as a fiddle and ready for love.

Now, one of the great sources for striking the third form of first blow arises when we try to save ourselves physical effort by getting others, without paying them, to do for us what we can do for ourselves. This occurs when we ask them to do us favors, which blames them in advance for refusing to do what is a euphemistic way of telling them what to do, and then, when they decide against it, we justify criticizing or hurting them in some way by claiming they struck the first blow because they didn't do what we judged they should. But when we know that though we have the right to ask favors, they have the right-of-way to refuse if they want to, for which we cannot desire to strike the third form of first blow because they will simply deny us greater satisfaction in this direction by turning the other cheek, we are forced to restrict our requests only to those things we cannot do for ourselves. It is true we cannot have sexual intercourse by ourselves, but it is within our power to arouse the desire of our partners to accept an invitation; therefore, this is something we can do for ourselves.

How many times do we carelessly forget to do something and then blame others in advance by asking them to do it for us? In our present world, should they refuse, we blame them because this means we have to do it. But when we know that we can no longer hurt them for refusing to do favors for us, we are compelled to think like never before to save ourselves unnecessary physical effort. More arguments have arisen because we are constantly judging what our partners should do, which starts a chain reaction of resentment because we then blame them, and they blame us for blaming them. When we understand what constitutes the third form of first blow and who has the right-of-way, arguments resulting from this source must come to a permanent end. But let us go a step further.

It is impossible to ask a favor without asking a question, which means that every time we ask a question, we are asking people to do us a favor and answer our question. But supposing we should ask, "When did Columbus discover America?" and they should tell us they don't know, whereupon we tell them. Isn't it obvious that the purpose of the question was to find out if we possess knowledge or information they don't, so that we can feel superior in this regard? Aren't we glad they didn't know? And if we blame them for not knowing, as teachers do to students, aren't we judging that this is something they should be aware of? But when we know that they are not going to laugh at us for asking questions, the answers of which are already known to us, and never blame us for trying to make them feel inferior or for criticizing them for this lack of knowledge, we are compelled to think like never before so as not to do those things that will make us appear foolish in our own eyes because there is no one we can blame. Remember, they have the right-of-way to refuse answering our questions because, to satisfy our desire, they must do something for us, whereas to satisfy their desire not to answer, there is not anything we have to do for them.

Now when a couple get married under the changed conditions, we will never tell our partners what to do except to remind them when they are striking a first blow. If a husband is the only one working, he will never tell his wife that it is her duty to do certain things, just as she would never tell him where or when to work or to give her money. However, she knows that if she wastes one penny by burning electricity that is not needed, as an example, she is striking a first blow for which he would never blame her, making it impossible for her to find satisfaction in being careless about these things. Because she knows that he would never tell her that it is her duty to prepare the meals, to keep the house clean, etc., as this is a judgment of what is right for her, she will do everything in her power to do what will make him happy, while he, knowing that it is not her duty to wash the dishes, clothes, make beds, etc., will dump his own garbage, wash his own plates, make his own bed, and see that she has enough money. Should he have extra money and wish to spend it on a maid to save her some physical effort, he would desire this all the more because he knows she would never ask. By the same reasoning, should she wish to take a job and bring in extra money to help her husband support the family, she would desire this all the more because he would never ask her to do this. The very fact that they will never ask favors of each other except in rare cases will compel them to ask each other if there is anything they can do and then not to take advantage of this generous offer because to do so would reveal their selfishness, not their love, they are forced to restrict their requests only to those things they know would be a pleasure for their partner to do for them.

When husbands and wives become citizens, the laws of their country will no longer play any role in their staying together, which means that if either wants to leave after all first blows are removed from their marriage, nothing will stop them but their own conscience. However, should a husband walk out regardless and make no effort to support his family, it is equivalent to him dying, as far as his wife is concerned, and she would immediately come under the guarantee if she has no reserve cash, no job, and no possibility of a job, which actually means that he cannot find greater satisfaction in leaving her if this can only be done at our expense. If he has enough money to support two families and can leave his wife because not to leave would make matters worse for himself, since he was already in love with another person when becoming a citizen, then he will be able to find greater satisfaction in so doing. But when she begins to apply the principles of the examination, he could very well fall in love with her all over again and decide not to leave after all.

As for those of us who are not sexually satisfied because our mates are committing adultery or just not in the mood to have sex with us (although they are not thinking of divorce), since we can no longer blame them, we must do everything in our power to arouse sexual desire without physical contact or obligation. But if our invitation is not accepted time and time again, it becomes a first blow that conscience will not allow to continue when all criticism is removed. Sooner or later, the people committing adultery will have to make some kind of adjustment because it will be difficult for them to reject a partner who would not only not criticize them for this or anything done but not blame them, no matter how much it hurts, even if adultery was committed right in view. Part of the excitement is in the deception (forbidden fruit is sweet) and in the higher degree of passion, but when a wife and husband know that the other will never blame anything, and when all arguments are removed because neither will ever tell the other what to do, they become somewhat like strangers where sex is concerned because no demands will be made. This in itself will arouse desire, but when they become extremely sexy because there is no other way to extend an invitation, and when they know they are completely free to have as many lovers as their conscience allows, you will see that even the atmosphere of the people already married when the transition begins will be forced in the direction of monogamy. As for widows, widowers, and divorced people, regardless of their age, they, too, can fall in love and therefore will be compelled to search for a mate they do not want to hurt. Chapter Five covers this.

For the very first time, newlyweds will know that no one would ever enter their home and complain about the way it was decorated, simply because this would be a first blow for which there would be no blame. This means that the need to compliment has seen its last days because it has no value unless there can be criticism, just as there can be nothing beautiful when there is nothing ugly. Consequently, furniture will be arranged as to what satisfies the individuals in that home, but if there is a conflict as to where something should be placed, they would flip a coin because both would desire to yield to the other since there are no more standards as to what is a better arrangement, which obviates the need to employ an interior decorator or ask the opinion of others.

As for what they do with their own time, this is also their business. If the husband has a desire to play pool, golf, or do any number of things while she desires to play canasta, bridge, bowl, or do any number of things, they will not stand in each other's way because this would be telling them what they can and cannot do, and they have the right-of-way to do what they judge to be right for themselves. However, if his wife does not have money to pay for a babysitter, he knows that she would never utter a word of criticism if he left her every night, but he cannot find greater satisfaction in keeping her back from satisfying her desires, which means that he would want to babysit himself so she could get out. If they can afford a babysitter, there is no standard that they must do things together. He might prefer to see The Hustler, a movie about pool playing, while she may desire to see a picture about having babies. He could extend her an invitation to join him, or she could extend one to join her, but what they decide to do is their business.

When he leaves for or returns from work, he is under no obligation, nor is she, to kiss or say certain things. They can do what they want, but the other has the right-of-way not to participate if this is desired. In our present world, if we approach our partners for a kiss or a hug and it is not returned, we blame them for not satisfying our desire. Perhaps our desire to hug and kiss those we love will never be rejected, but if it is, we must remember that they have the right-of-way, and if we criticize them, we are revealing our selfishness, not our love, and striking the third form of first blow for which they will never blame us.

This right-of-way system will permit many customs, conventions, and habits to be broken without being criticized. How many times have we been judged in the wrong for not desiring to return a kiss, a handshake, or a verbal salutation? This does not mean that we have to stop doing what we have always done where others are concerned, just as long as they desire the same thing. But if they don't, and we cannot force them to do what they do not want to do without striking a first blow, which cannot be preferred under the changed conditions, we are given no choice but to change our ways.

If a wife is in the mood for love because she has been daydreaming about her last episode, nothing is preventing her from slipping into, or saying something sexy to arouse his desire to accept her invitation the moment he comes home from work, which tells him immediately what she wants without imposing an obligation. If this does not put him in the mood, she will never blame him, but after a hot bath and dinner, he may decide to slip into something sexy and extend her an invitation, which she would never refuse, although he could just wrap his arms around her since she already expressed her desire. In our present world, the wife would punish her husband by refusing him because he refused her, and an argument would start. Should he not wish to wait until after dinner because he, too, was daydreaming and impatient to extend an invitation, they could have sex right then and there, but how and where they make love is their business. There is no such thing as a perverted act in the new world. They cannot force the other to do what is not desired, but they will find out what makes the other extremely passionate and then move in that direction for greater satisfaction.

CHAPTER ELEVEN
PARENTS AND CHILDREN

THE NEXT HURT TO BE removed is that which we have been striking our children not because they violated a rule, regulation, commandment, standard, or law that tries to prevent them from making matters worse for ourselves, but only because they didn't agree with our judgment of what is better for them; and we justified this third form of first blow by calling it punishment. But when we become citizens and fully realize that they have the right-of-way to do anything that does not make matters worse for us, we are forced to arouse their desire to move in the direction we prefer without resorting to this blow to accomplish our purpose. However, just as noncitizens will continue to be punished should they be caught violating any laws (which is done as the lesser of two evils until they pass their examination), so will children if they know that breaking any rules will make matters worse for us. But when the injustice of the third form of first blow is removed that forces them to do what they have the right-of-way not to do, and when they are taught the basic principle, they will never be able to find greater satisfaction in disobeying those regulations that represent first blows. Now let me clarify this by observing them being raised under the changed conditions which will bring about, out of absolute necessity, the greatest filial and parental love possible.

When they are very young, we rarely consider their desire at all, only what we believe is better for them. Consequently, if they push away certain food, we blame them for not eating it. In our mind, there are certain beliefs that control our thinking. Carrots are good for the eyes, while spinach will build muscle. If they don't eat enough (what we judge this to be), they will get underweight, undernourished, sick, and need a doctor. To prevent all this, we push them to eat what they don't like the taste of. But when we know that they cannot be blamed for disliking what food we think is for their benefit or for liking what we believe is not for their welfare, we are compelled to prepare and combine their food in such a manner that they will not reject what we want them to eat. But if they should, there is nothing we can do except to find out what other food they do like, unless we prefer to force into their system what they don't like by making it the lesser of two evils, since the other alternative is starvation. This means that all the values we have been using to guide our decisions, providing there is a conflict, must yield to their values, but as a result, they will grow and develop like animals who are not forced to eat when not hungry and what is not liked. Most babies will grow and develop in spite of, not because of the kind of food given, simply because the body is very tough and capable of adjusting to most conditions. This in itself is not a sufficient reason to feed them anything, but there is another reason which prevents us from so doing because it makes matters worse for ourselves.

When they are born their stomach has never had any food at all, so it is possible that if mother's milk is not used since it developed with them (or even after they are weaned, should we push into it what they really don't want), they could get all kinds of cramps, indigestion, colic, etc. Now, if this should happen, the only way they can express their feelings is by screaming or crying. Most of us have experienced this to a degree that was almost unbearable and at a time that was inconvenient. We were asleep for the night or making love. How many times have we, not knowing what else to do, preferred to walk, rock, or bounce them around until the screaming stopped? This not only was an annoyance in itself, but right here is the origin of spoiling, which is a habit, not good or bad in itself, that we start and then blame them for. Before long, the pain subsides and they fall asleep, but this wonderful feeling of being bounced around is remembered, and they know that it occurs only when they scream at the top of their lungs. Soon they scream not because they're in pain but only to get us to give them that wonderful feeling again. However, when we are compelled to give them what they prefer in the way of milk and other food, it appears that the chances of stomach pains are less likely to occur, and should they sleep soundly through the night, then the conditions that compelled us to select the lesser of two evils, that is, this rocking and bouncing to stop the screaming, never arise. But if they are already spoiled and we know they are crying to make us do what we prefer not to do, just remember that we have the right-of-way because they need us to satisfy their desire and should let them scream until they realize that we cannot be controlled by their crying. If we are in doubt as to the reason for their crying, and it gives us greater satisfaction to comfort them by holding them in our arms, who is there to tell us this is wrong? We have a perfect right to raise them as we please, even spoil them if this is our preference, but should they become intolerable monsters who make us yield as the lesser of two evils, we have nobody to blame but ourselves when they can no longer be blamed for what is our responsibility.

If we wish them to be in bed at a certain time, this is also our business, but if we can't justify punishing them for not going to bed because this is not a first blow and the only way it might be possible to make them healthy, wealthy, and wise is to sacrifice our desire to watch a television show so they will imitate us, we might soon be compelled to believe that early to bed and early to rise is not so vitally important. If we feel that staying up beyond a certain time might make them so tired the next day that they won't want to go to school, you are jumping to a premature conclusion because this is impossible just as long as staying home will give them less satisfaction. However, because being tired might make them enjoy school less, and because going to school will be such a fantastic pleasure under the changed conditions, as you will soon see, they might prefer to go to bed early so they can enjoy school more by not being tired. But whatever they choose to do is their business, not ours, just as long as they are not hurting us.

If we want them to do chores without being paid in some way, we must develop the habit so it becomes their responsibility because they have the right-of-way and are not striking a first blow by not doing what we want done; therefore, we cannot justify punishment, although we can strike the third form of first blow if our conscience will allow it. Should we prefer to reward them for satisfying our desires, remember that they have the right-of-way to stop doing what we want done should they prefer to sacrifice what we are paying them, or to ask for more if they feel we are not paying enough. If we don't accept their terms, we must sacrifice whatever we were paying them to do, so we must be very careful about starting habits for which we can never blame them. Doing chores will become a second nature when the habit is developed; and when they are old enough to understand that they are helping reduce our physical effort for which we would never blame them if they stopped what has become their responsibility, even if this meant we would have to work harder ourselves, they would soon prefer to continue helping us because not to would give them less satisfaction. However, asking favors is an altogether different thing and cannot be placed in the same category as chores; otherwise, we could take advantage by making them feel guilty by not blaming them for refusing to do what we have requested.

"Honey, would you mind running downstairs and getting Daddy the evening paper?"

"Not now, Daddy; I'm busy."

"That's all right, sweetheart, you don't have to do it if you don't want to. I'll get it myself even though I'm so tired."

His daughter, suddenly feeling responsible for the possibility of hurting her father, then answers reluctantly, "Never mind, Daddy, I'll get it for you."

But when we know that they have the right-of-way to refuse what we have the right to ask, we can no longer justify making them feel guilty over not doing it, which forces us not to be careless about forgetting to do certain things that will make us work harder simply because we can no longer desire to hurt them or make them feel guilty for not doing what we should have done for ourselves or for doing what they have the right-of-way to do.

Now the next thing demanded by our conscience is that we treat every person in the world with equal respect, which is denied by words that make certain people (their physiognomies, pursuits, and abilities) superior productions of the human race. You have seen that no one is beautiful or ugly, but who will believe that no one is educated, uneducated, intelligent, or unintelligent. However, before you jump to any conclusions, let me explain certain facts.

Bearing in mind that nothing of value can exist in the external world except in relation to someone, the word education implies the existence of something that contains an intrinsic value, and the more of it we acquire, the more educated and valuable we become, which means that those who do not partake of it will be judged uneducated and of lesser value. If someone drops out of school, he is not as educated as the individual who graduates, nor is this graduate as educated as a college dropout who is less educated than the Ph.D. who is less educated than a professor. As a consequence of this external value, we are treated with greater respect the more of it we acquire. Certain diplomas exact the title of doctor, which requires that these Ph.D.s look down on us with less respect than is given to them, and someone who never learned to read or write is made to feel as if he is an absolute nonentity. It is difficult for him to hold up his head in the presence of these educated giants. But Will Durant, having gone far beyond these professors in his mental development, resented the preemption of education by the colleges and defined it in a way to include those who did not finish school but continued to read and study on their own, which made the universities dislike him, while the dropouts loved him. To him, education was a definite reality, something of great value. He didn't realize he was dealing only in words. It is absolutely true that someone who has learned certain things will prove more valuable to a corporation that requires this knowledge, just as certain features will prove more valuable to a movie studio, but this doesn't make him of any greater value intrinsically. If he desires to read 10,000 books and go to school for 20 years, this is his business, but it does not make him any more educated than a particular physiognomy will make him handsome. He is actually different than the person who never went to school, never read a book, and fished for 20 years, but this does not entitle him to more respect, which is what takes place when the word educated projects this value into individuals whose existence cannot be denied. For the very first time in history, we are going to be compelled to mind our own business for greater satisfaction, which was denied by words like beautiful and educated since these were a judgment by us of what was better for others. Removing all the synonyms and antonyms of the word educated doesn't mean that they will lose their desire to go to school, because what they prefer to do with their time is conditioned by what they want to become, but it does mean that they will never again be shown less respect, no matter what they look like or what they desire or do not desire to study.

As for the word intelligent and all its antonyms, we set up certain tests to determine the I.Q. of our children, and then, because some of them are unable to do as well, we call them less intelligent. But in reality, the only thing we really know when the word intelligent is removed is that some people can do certain things better than others, which is an undeniable fact.

Supposing we used the ability to play pool, golf, and chess as a test to determine the I.Q. of our professors and then graded them as to how well they did against the champions of the world in those fields. Wouldn't we call most of them very unintelligent if other beginners did much better? Can't you see now that the most we can say is that these professors cannot play these games as well, just as the champions of the world cannot do as well as the professors in their fields. By removing the words intelligent, educated, and beautiful, we are not showing any disrespect to the people these words were directed to by judging them an inferior production of the human race, but by removing all the antonyms, we raise those who were judged an inferior production to an absolute level of respect and equality, except in their ability to do certain things.

We teach children to call us dad, mom, uncle, and aunt, which we certainly have the right to do. But when they call us by our first name, we criticize them when they have done absolutely nothing to hurt us. This does not mean it is wrong to develop the habit of having them call us by these terms, but if they should ever decide to address us by our first names, this is their right-of-way and not a sign of disrespect, whereas our criticism of them is not showing them respect.

It is true that when we become accustomed to being addressed a certain way, it feels strange when this is suddenly changed, but this does not make it disrespectful. Are you beginning to see how unjust we have always been out of necessity? But in reality, all of us are perfectly equal in intrinsic value, and the knowledge of our true nature and who has the right-of-way forces us, for the very first time, to treat each other as equals, that is, not with lesser or greater respect.

The hurt in human relations, minding other people's business, trying to force them to do what they don't want to do, criticizing their behavior, asking certain type favors and questions and all the rest, comes to an end not because these things are wrong (we have the right to do anything we want, if we want to), not because of ethical or moral principles, the Ten Commandments, the laws of a nation, customs, conventions, tradition, etiquette, the teachings in the Bible, the belief in God, or anything else you care to throw in, but only because we cannot find greater satisfaction (the direction we are compelled to go) in continuing to do these things when we become citizens and understand the undeniable truth about our nature.

SEYMOUR LESSANS

CHAPTER TWELVE
TEACHERS AND STUDENTS

JUST AS WE WILL NEVER pass judgment on whether people are sufficiently trained to drive a motor vehicle without hurting us, because this is their business, not ours, so will we, as teachers, never pass judgment on whether our students are sufficiently trained to leave school and drive their profession or career, whatever you wish to call it, through the traffic of the economic world without hurting us, because this, too, is their business. This means very simply that there will be no more graduations, diplomas, or titles because this indicates that we have judged them qualified, whereas they will remain in school until they judge themselves qualified according to whatever standards the school has available. But there are certain fields, the knowledge is not yet available for the school to set up any such standard. In other words, when taking their final examination, which will be the completest and toughest ever given and may take several days or even weeks (the teacher will simply mark their test and return it with the answers so they can judge for themselves whether they are ready to leave school and enter the economic world), how is it possible for them to desire cheating under these conditions? Remember, they can leave school at any time and pretend to their employer that they are adequately trained to do what he would be paying them for, but should they make mistakes that hurt him, they will know that he can never blame them because the responsibility was his since he hired them, which deprives them of any satisfaction in being excused for pretending to him that they were adequately trained when they know they were not. This forces them to learn all that school has to teach regarding the career selected so that if mistakes are made, it would be through carelessness, which must also come to an end, or simply because there isn't any knowledge available to prevent what happened except by not taking on the risk, as was explained in relation to doctors. This places the full responsibility of when our students leave college not on whether they get a passing mark, for there will be no such thing, but strictly on whether they are satisfied with the results of their test. This also means there will be no more dropouts as such because every student will drop out sooner or later, but the reason for their leaving will be nobody's business but their own. There will be no more college graduates, no more educated, uneducated, intelligent, unintelligent, beautiful, or ugly individuals in the world, just people who will be doing something from day to day as they are compelled to move in the direction of greater satisfaction.

We will completely cease asking students verbal questions, the answers of which are already known to us, because this can only be done to find out if they know what we think they should, and what they know or don't know is not our business unless we are using the results of a test to determine their qualifications for a particular job or unless they have not yet become citizens and are still too young to assume responsibility for themselves, which does not take away from the fact that we must assume responsibility for everybody we employ.

If they should give wrong answers in any of the written tests we give them as teachers, they have the right-of-way to question us about anything they do not understand because they are paying us to teach them. If we are swamped with questions which we cannot desire to criticize, the only way we can prevent this is by making everything so clear that there will never be any need for these questions. However, we have the right-of-way to set up what time we would like a class to begin, and the fact that we would never blame students who are late and who, as a consequence, would be forced to ask unnecessary questions had they not fallen behind in their studies compels them to desire being on time because they cannot get greater satisfaction in being excused for making us work harder than it is necessary. We also have the right-of-way to set what mark we require for them to pass to a higher grade, which means that should they fail this test, they do not have the right-of-way to pass to the next grade, although they could enter this new class if they want to. But when they realize that they might not be able to keep up with the other students, which would cause us to work harder by the necessary questions they would be forced to ask, they would rather study harder before taking the test they failed so they could enter the next grade with the knowledge that they are able to keep up with the other students and not be an unnecessary burden to us. Besides, of what advantage is entering the next grade without the required mark when in the final examination before leaving school, should they not be satisfied with the results, they would never desire to accept a position doing what they know they are not completely qualified for when they also know that their employer must excuse any mistakes they make, which they can never justify.

Homework, for the very first time, will not be something they have to do but will want to do because they will never accomplish their purpose otherwise. We will still assign them certain books and pages to be studied in preparation for a test, but they will never have to prepare a paper or write a thesis that will be judged according to our personal standards when this has no relation whatsoever to the facts it is necessary for them to know in order to earn a living. However, we will be completely free to teach what we want to teach, but they will have the right-of-way to learn what they want to be taught, which means that they can reject what we might recommend.

If we, as parents, do not have or do not wish to spend the money for our children to go to college, they will be able to borrow the amount needed, without interest, from the guarantee, even before they have attained a standard of living. What they earn for a full year after leaving school will determine the amount we will guarantee, and they will pay back what was borrowed by remitting everything in excess of that amount. But should they improve their standard of living far beyond what it was the first year of their career, the guarantee only applies to the original figure should they ever be forced to go back down. The fact that they will be able to borrow this money obviates the need to ask us to do for them what they can do for themselves.

BEYOND THE FRAMEWORK OF MODERN THOUGHT

IN CONCLUDING THIS work, I shall quote and then paraphrase Will Durant on education, which word, of course, must come to an end. He writes: "I believe that it is through reading, rather than through high school and college, that we at last acquire a liberal education. Today we think a man is educated if he can read the newspapers morning, noon and night; but though our colleges turn out graduates like so many standardized Fords every year, there is a visible dearth of real culture in our life; we are a nation with a hundred thousand schools, and hardly a dozen educated men. Education should make a man complete; it should develop every creative power in him, and open his mind to all the enjoyable and instructive aspects of the world. A man who is heavy with millions but to whom Beethoven or Corot or Hardy, or the glow of the autumn woods in the setting sun, is only sound and color signifying nothing, is merely the raw material of a man; half the world is closed to the blurred windows of his spirit.

Education does not mean that we have become certified experts in business, or mining, or botany, or journalism, or epistemology; it means that through the absorption of the moral, intellectual and esthetic inheritance of our race we have come to understand and control ourselves as well as the external world; that we have chosen the best as our associates both in spirit and in the flesh; that we have learned to add courtesy to culture, wisdom to knowledge, and forgiveness to understanding. When will our colleges produce such men?"

However this may be from Durant's point of view, in the new world, "we are able to control and understand ourselves as well as the external world," not because we have absorbed the "moral, intellectual, and esthetic inheritance of our race," but only because we know what it means that our eyes are not a sense organ, that our will is not free, and why there is nothing to fear in death. "We have chosen the best as our associates both in spirit and in the flesh," only because the knowledge that we will never be criticized or ridiculed allows us, for the very first time, to select what is truly best for ourselves, even though we may prefer the Beatles to Beethoven, Zane Grey to Shakespeare, Elvis Presley to Caruso, the atmosphere of a pool hall to the "glow of the autumn woods in the setting sun," or a garbage collector for a friend to an author, philosopher, historian, or piano virtuoso. "We have learned to add courtesy to culture and wisdom to knowledge" only because we have really learned to mind our own business, learned what respect is, learned that all mankind are perfectly equal in intrinsic value, and learned how unconsciously ignorant of the truth we have always been, which wisdom makes it impossible to be discourteous when there is no culture, no education, no beauty, and no other words to make us feel that we are an inferior production of the human race. And we have added "forgiveness to understanding" only because we know at last that man is truly not to blame, which gives us the understanding to prevent from coming back that for which forgiveness was previously necessary. "When will our colleges produce such men?" Only when we pass the examination and become citizens of this new world.

POSTSCRIPT

Sadly, the author passed away in 1991 at the age of 72. Although he tried to reach scientists who could validate his findings, he was unable to get anyone to listen because he was not a member of a leading university and held no distinguishing titles. As a consequence, this knowledge has never been widely distributed, nor has it been given a thorough investigation.

Would you kindly take a moment to give this book a positive review? This will help in our effort to bring this major discovery to light. The audio that goes along with this book offers further clarification regarding the basic principle and its extension. As mentioned, you can listen to the author as he reads and elaborates on Chapter One. Just copy the link below and scroll down.

Thank you.

www.declineandfallofallevil.com/ebook[1]

www.facebook.com/DeterminismandConscience[2]

---

1.   http://www.declineandfallofallevil.com/ebook

2.   https://www.facebook.com/DeterminismandConscience/

Did you love *Beyond the Framework of Modern Thought*? Then you should read *This Is An Urgent Message From A Visitor To Your Planet*[3] by Seymour Lessans and Ruomyes Snassel!

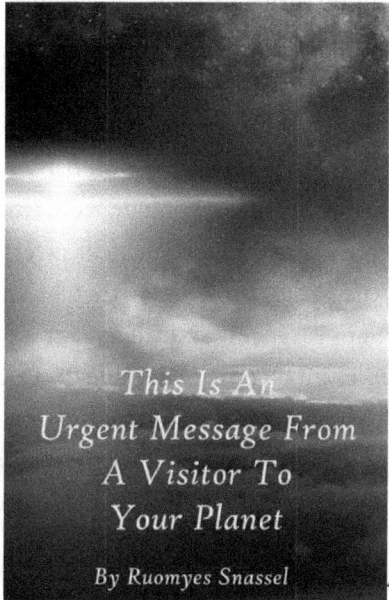

Our visitor reveals, in the first few pages, the reason their GREAT TRANSITION was delayed 500 years, and a similar thing could happenhere because we have also been taught to believe, through words that do not symbolize reality but give the appearance of doing so, that a certain aspect of man's nature is absolutely true. As a consequence, the natural, psychological law hidden behind the door stating that this "aspect of man's nature" is false, could remain permanently concealed because

3. https://books2read.com/u/31x0X6

4. https://books2read.com/u/31x0X6

our leading authorities, the very people who don't know the truth but think they do, may never desire to open that door for a thorough investigation when the claim of what can be accomplished appears ridiculous, impossible, and compromises the integrity of their knowledge and capabiity. If they can't solve our problems, and they are the experts, it stands to reason that no one else can. However, if you will bear in mind how many times in the course of history has the IMPOSSIBLE (that which appeared to be) been made possible by a scientific breakthrough, you will refrain from jumping to a premature conclusion, will give this VISITOR the benefit of the doubt, will open that hermetically sealed door in spite of appearances, and then, after a complete study of all the principles involved, will be able to see that our NEW WORLD must become a reality sooner or later and could take place within the 21st century, if this natural law is released from its hiding place quickly enough and thoroughly understood.

Also by Seymour Lessans

Watch for more at www.declineandfallofallevil.com.